G000243777

Victorian and Edwardian Houses

A Guide to Care and Maintenance

Victorian and Edwardian Houses

A Guide to Care and Maintenance

Janet Collings

THE CROWOOD PRESS

First published in 2008 by
The Crowood Press Ltd
Ramsbury, Marlborough
Wiltshire SN8 2HR

www.crowood.com

British Library Cataloguing-in-Publication Data
A catalogue record for this book is available from the British Library.

ISBN 978 1 84797 057 2

Disclaimer
The techniques and materials referred to in this book are part of a continually developing understanding of practical conservation in the United Kingdom. The demands of sustainable living and climate change may develop in ways that cannot reasonably be anticipated within the scope of this book. Regulations and laws can differ across the United Kingdom and may also be subject to change over time. The information here is generic, it cannot relate to every building or every circumstance and is not a substitute for professional or technical advice. The author and publisher do not accept liability for any error or omission. It is not possible to refer here to every relevant organization or website, there may be others of equal merit and those mentioned are referred to in good faith but with no responsibility for their conduct or content. The author and publisher have no control over how the information in the book is used and can accept no liability for any loss, damage or injury however caused.

Frontispiece: The Victorian and Edwardian period saw houses beginning to move away from using completely local building materials and also the increased use of decorative embellishments.

Designed and typeset by Focus Publishing, Sevenoaks, Kent

Printed and bound in Singapore by Craft Print International Ltd

Contents

DEDICATION

To my parents who supported my ambition
to become an architect from an early age.

ACKNOWLEDGEMENTS

To all the houses and the people who have helped to make this book, and with special thanks to those who have opened their rooms to the camera.

Introduction

This book is for owners of houses that were built between about 1840 and 1914 and aims to help them to become responsible custodians for the future. This book focuses on retaining the fabric of the existing house, as this allows more of the past to be preserved and is also a sustainable approach. This may also save money and time by outlining the least wasteful way of looking after the house, and is also likely to enhance the value by keeping its period appeal.

The subjects covered here range from the historical context to how to approach conservation. This is followed by a detailed examination of the types of material and decoration used for the exterior and interior of the house and how repairs can be approached. The setting of the house is then looked at before alterations and extensions are considered. This is followed by an explanation of energy conservation measures, a maintenance checklist and, finally, some common mistakes to try to avoid with Victorian and Edwardian houses.

CHAPTER 1

History, Research and Legal

HISTORICAL CONTEXT

The period covered by this book saw a great expansion in house building to provide for the rising urban population. This meant that an enormous number of houses had to be constructed. Large quantities of building materials were required and, if local sources were in short supply, then materials had to be transported from further away. Greater industrialization of the building industry began with the creation and expansion of the canal network from the late eighteenth century onwards. Before this horse-drawn transport was used to convey materials to where they were needed and, where rivers were nearby, they enabled them to be transported further. This meant that buildings tended to be constructed from locally-grown or hand-made building materials. The creation of most of the railway network between 1833 and 1853 enabled stone, slates and bricks to be used in those parts of the country where they had not been previously available. Pattern books and trade catalogues from this period illustrate the wide range of building products and designs that were available to builders when they were constructing houses. Since many houses were rented rather than owned during this period there was competition between

This group of houses appears little altered since its construction and may offer some interesting insights into why and for whom they were built.

builders to secure tenants. This often meant that as many decorative architectural features as possible were incorporated within a house to make it more desirable to rent than other houses in the locality.

Victorian houses were often constructed on the outskirts of existing towns and villages. On roads leading out of towns it is often quite easy to see where the building of Victorian houses started and then further developed through the Edwardian era. The types of house built much depended on the area, local demand and land ownership. Individual villas set in the middle of a plot may have had carefully considered architectural embellishments, while pairs of semi-detached houses were often designed to look more like larger houses.

Houses built at slightly different dates from each other may also have been subject to different design ideas or regulations. To maintain the architectural rhythm of a terrace of houses, where flats were being introduced, they usually had double-entry doors, often recessed under a porch, so that they looked more like single houses from the street. A later development in the Edwardian period was the mansion block. This allowed more flats to be incorporated on to a smaller piece of land, where building land was at a premium. The communal staircases often incorporated tiled dados and stained glass in the doors to the individual flats to make the properties more desirable to tenants.

Bay windows are typical of the period.

RESEARCHING THE HISTORY OF THE HOUSE

The legal documents connected with a house purchase are usually a good starting point for future research. Clues about the history or the area may be gained by looking at the house and its features. Check cupboards and difficult to find places since some useful historical information, such as decorating bills, may be discovered. If there are features that appear inconsistent or have been altered, this might help to explain how or why the house has developed in the way that it has. Comparing similarities and differences with other houses in the area may also provide useful background information. In addition, speak to anyone who has known the area for some time. If there is a local history society it may

This estate cottage appears to have been little altered since it was built.

Researching the history of houses may reveal many interesting facts about their history and development.

Where a terrace of houses was being built there was ample opportunity to make the facades more interesting by incorporating different sizes of house within the group.

have useful archival information. Local publications may be available, such as books or picture postcards. The Internet is also likely to play a significant role as there may be images, maps and historical information that can be searched. Historical maps may also be found for particular areas, such as Charles Booth's maps of London. The local authority usually has an archive or local studies department and there may also be a county records office with books, maps or old directories for the area.

LEGAL STATUS

While there are many Victorian and Edwardian houses that may be listed or within conservation areas, many houses from this time may not be covered by these designations. However, the latter form a valuable part of the architectural heritage of the country. For this reason it is prudent to treat all houses with the same level of respect as listed buildings so that future generations will be able to appreciate their

This Suffolk house has a slate roof that would have been transported by rail from Wales. Due to the county's geology, it does not have any natural stone or slate, however, the local clays meant that brick-making skills were highly developed from an early date.

Villas such as this have a substantial bay window feature, a popular embellishment of the period.

This terrace of cottages has been little altered over the years and still retains the original cast-iron railings that were made at the local iron foundry.

Only the division in the roof hints at how these houses have been subdivided.

This individual house retains many of its original features.

Where there are different architectural styles within a row of houses it may indicate that there was a change of land ownership or that the houses were built under different building regulations. In this example the three-storey house on the left has a semi-basement unlike the two-storey houses on the right. Often by looking at old maps of the area from different dates it may be possible to establish which pieces of land had been developed and by which date.

The front doors of these houses are equally spaced. They have parapet walls to the house fronts, which indicates that they have butterfly roofs behind.

The rear elevation of a butterfly roof; at the front the roof line would often be concealed behind a parapet.

These houses have mirrored house plans since the front doors are grouped in pairs.

These houses also have mirrored house plans because the front doors are adjacent.

history and architectural features. Alterations and extensions inevitably change the character of a house, so buying one that meets one's current requirements rather than making alterations is a more sensitive and sustainable approach, as the original fabric of the house will not be lost in the process.

Conservation Areas

Conservation areas range in size from village centres to areas of historic street patterns within towns and cities. In all cases, these areas include buildings of architectural and historical merit. In addition, some buildings in conservation areas may also be listed. Where the local authority has designated a conservation area, additional planning constraints are in place. This is to protect the environment from unsympathetic alterations or developments that may detract from the overall character or appearance of the area. Alterations to, principally, the public face of any buildings within a conservation area are likely to require permission before any works are carried out. Details of conservation areas may be found on the

Where the house plans are mirrored between pairs of houses, the rear extensions can be paired together under one single roof.

A typical example of a rear elevation for a pair of houses.

These arches each incorporate two doors to flats.

An Edwardian mansion block.

local authority's website or by speaking to the planning department. Within conservation areas trees are also protected, so that the local authority has to be notified in writing in advance of any proposed pruning, lopping or felling. In some conservation areas specific additional conditions apply because of the architectural importance or historical interest of certain features such as windows, doors, railings, walls or fences that may be significant among the particular merits of the area.

LISTED BUILDINGS

Some Victorian and Edwardian houses are listed. In these cases the listing description is available either on the Internet (*see* websites) or from the local authority. Listed buildings are currently identified in three categories in England and Wales. Grade I is the highest one that contains a very small number of the most special buildings. Grade II* is the second highest category with a slightly greater number of

The original integrity of this street can still be read, even though some houses have slightly different colour schemes.

Researching the history of these houses would explain why some have dormer windows in the roofs and others appear to have been built without them.

significant buildings. However, by far the largest category is Grade II that contains the majority of listed buildings in England and Wales. In Scotland buildings are divided into categories rather than into grades, where A is the highest, followed by B and C(s). In Northern Ireland the grades are A (again the highest), B+ and Grade B (1 and 2). In addition to statutory listed buildings, local authorities also have lists of locally listed buildings. These buildings are taken into consideration when planning applications are being considered that may affect them or their setting. Currently PPG15 (Planning Policy Guidance 15: Planning and the historic environment) is the basis for the care of listed buildings in England (*see* websites). Where a house is listed all parts of it are covered by that listing, whether specifically mentioned or not and both internally and externally. This listing may even extend to parts of the house that might be considered movable (for example, sculptures) if they contribute to the overall architectural merit of the house. In addition, where a house is listed, buildings or other items that are considered to be within the 'curtilage' of the house (the area around the house or that is considered to be a part of the setting) may also be listed. The extent of this area may be confirmed with the conservation officer at the local authority and may not necessarily conform to current ownership boundaries.

Start by looking at the house and its surroundings, which may indicate directions for research. Where a new road or street was developed the name of the road may be significant in connection with the history of the house or reveal the developer's ideas about the initial market for the houses.

This inscription written on a plastered wall by a decorator is dated 1875 and was found where later layers of wallpaper had come away from the wall.

CHAPTER 2

Conservation Philosophy

Owners of Victorian and Edwardian homes are their custodians for a relatively short period in the life of the houses. This means that owners have a responsibility to ensure that the original features are retained for the next occupants to appreciate. Owning an older house is about accepting compromise as things are never perfect. This also requires a certain amount of flexibility on the part of the occupants to adjust to living in them. This is because a certain amount of weathering or general wear and tear, that is also sometimes referred to as 'pleasing decay' or 'the patina of age', has to be acceptable to the owners as being part of their responsibility. The delicate balance in looking after an older house is to decide the point at which pleasing decay has evolved into the need to carry out some minimal and sympathetic repairs that do not detract from the house or try to turn it into a new one. In recent decades there has been a presumption towards thinking that the best way to care for an older house was to 'gut' it and start again, but this is no longer a responsible attitude. That approach not only destroys many of the original features, but it also wastes existing materials that contain embodied energy and consumes many more new materials during renewal works.

The beauty of this terrace is due to its uniformity.

CONSERVATION PHILOSOPHY

Where repairs to the fabric are considered appropriate, the philosophy to use is one of minimal intervention and to retain as much of the existing fabric as possible. Both these approaches are also very sustainable. When working with older houses it can be more appropriate to use the same traditional materials that were used when the house was constructed, so that problems of incompatibility are avoided. Many recently developed materials have yet to be fully understood and sometimes it may be many years before their full characteristics are known.

Glossary

Care and conservation are about looking after an old house in a sympathetic way, which means aiming to retain all of the original fabric. Where repairs are necessary, the minimal amount of fabric should be removed in order to carry out the repair.

Compatibility is using building materials that are similar to the ones used when the house was built so that they behave in the same way. Often using modern building materials in an older house can create problems since they may behave differently.

Minimum intervention is disturbing or removing as little as possible of the original fabric when carrying out repairs to either the house or its surroundings.

Embodied energy is the amount of energy used to create and transport a building material to where it is to be used and is therefore also the amount of energy already bound up in the manufacture, installation and maintenance of an existing feature.

Environmentally friendly should mean the use of new materials that have been produced by using low levels of energy and that have been transported only short distances to reduce energy consumption, but often this term is used to mean that products are supposed to be non-harmful or are energy efficient once in use.

Traditional construction refers to materials and techniques that were available when the house was constructed.

Artificial stone features were often originally left unpainted.

Reversibility is applicable where repairs, alterations and extensions are designed to be removable without leaving any scar, so that, if a later owner wishes to make changes, they will be able to do so as the original fabric of the house will have been retained unharmed.

Restoration implies that a house has been altered or taken back to a time for which accurate historical records may not be available; in addition, this usually means that more work and new materials are involved during this process, which is not being environmentally responsible.

Renovation implies that a house has been gutted before modern and often incompatible materials were put back and the original character and fabric of the house lost.

Sustainability is demonstrated where every decision about introducing new materials into a house has

As the original bricks and artificial stonework around the door and windows have not been painted on the middle house for a number of years, then, by default, the surface is more able to breathe than the houses on either side, which have had plastic-based masonry paint applied to the stone dressings.

been carefully considered as to whether it was absolutely necessary and also making sure that, where new materials were introduced, they have consumed as little energy and resources in their manufacture, transportation and use as possible.

Breathability

Victorian and Edwardian houses were often designed like older houses to allow any water that entered into its fabric, such as into the bricks or stone of the walls, to evaporate out. In addition, there may have been precautions incorporated into the structure, such as slate damp-proof courses at the base of the external walls, to stop damp rising up the walls. The prime aim was that any water that found its way into the house would be able to evaporate out again. Current construction methods and materials adopt a different approach and that is to seal up the fabric so that dampness of any sort cannot get in. Both construction methods and materials are appropriate to their own type of building construction; however, there are problems when current building techniques are applied to older houses. There are two specific areas where problems may arise: with the use of plastic-based masonry paints on external walls and the use of cement in mortar mixes for repointing brick and stonework, where the original mortar was a mix of sand and lime (*see* below).

Modern masonry paints are generally 'plastic'-based paints made from resins. These formulas have become almost universal for most paints that are used on brick and stone walls (hence they are known as masonry paints). As long as the plastic paint film is continuous, the underlying masonry surfaces remain protected from rain. Where the film deteriorates or is torn by movement and starts to split – because it is not as flexible as the background material it has been applied to – then water may be able to get in behind the paint. Because the paint is impervious, any trapped water is unable to evaporate and over time this starts to cause the fabric to decay. In addition, water vapour may also have entered the wall from other sources, such as the ground or from condensation within the building, this damp is also unable to evaporate through the skin of plastic paint. When this happens the water content starts to rise and this creates the ideal environment for wood-boring beetles to attack any timbers that are embedded in a masonry wall. Where the water content increases further rot may also become established.

Where masonry walls become damp, the bricks or stones may start to disintegrate or 'spall'. This is because the damp masonry may be subject to frost and pieces of the brick or stone are levered away from the background by expanding ice crystals. One way of dealing with some of these problems is to make sure that even the tiniest hairline splits or cracks in these types of paint are redecorated on a regular basis, so that rainwater at least does not get into the fabric of the house. The other more environmentally friendly approach is to use breathable paints as these allow any water that gets into the fabric to dry out, but to be effective they cannot be applied over any existing impervious paints, so those must be removed, which is often possible (*see* Chapter 3).

On external timberwork modern gloss paints are usually oil-alkyd-based, which also means that they have impervious qualities. The problem is that these types of paint finish also tend to split when the underlying timber expands and contracts during the seasons. These paints have taken over from lead-based paints which (although now banned from use on all but the higher grades of listed buildings) did have one very important quality and that was that they were a relatively flexible but, more importantly, that they allowed the timber to 'breathe' or to be able to dry out when wet. There are now greater ranges of more breathable paints available to the homeowner. One such is linseed oil paint and this is a close modern equivalent of the old-fashioned lead paint. One drawback with this type of paint is that some manufacturers recommend that any earlier layers of paint should be removed first in order to obtain the full benefits of the new paints. While this would allow for improved breathability, this would also destroy the historical layers of paint.

Modern eggshell and emulsion paints that are used on internal walls often contain plastic-based ingredients ('acrylic', 'vinyl') in them, which again means that any damp that gets into the wall is usually unable to evaporate. There are modern emulsion paints that are slightly more permeable, such as those used on newly plastered modern walls, but the use of traditional paints such as distempers, that are chalk-based, is perhaps a more appropriate option. Traditionally, ceilings and walls were painted with distemper as this is a more breathable finish, so, ideally, it would be good to return to the use of such types of paint.

Some houses were constructed by using cement mortars during this period, while others were built with traditional and breathable lime-based mortars, so the concept of breathability has to be assessed for each house individually. Problems may occur where cement mortars have been used to replace lime-based mortars. Cement is a relatively brittle and inflexible material, so, where it has been used in mortars around bricks or stones, it is not able to move at the same rate over the seasons. The consequence is that the mortar begins to crack. (This is the reason why expansion joints are incorporated into the design of new brickwork; these are vertical joints between maximum-sized areas of brickwork, the vertical joint is filled with an expandable, usually mastic, material to take up the movement between the two rigid panels of brickwork.)

When rainwater finds its way into cracked, cement-mortared brickwork it is unable to dry out, as another quality of cement is that it is relatively impervious. The trapped water then starts to attack the masonry that the cement was meant to be helping. The effect is usually that the face of the bricks or stones begins to flake away. The way to avoid these problems is to use mortar or render (external plaster) mixes that contain only lime and sand, which create a mix that is also slightly flexible. Typically, a lime mortar or render mix is roughly three parts of sand to one of lime. In addition, because the mortar is flexible it does not crack the surrounding bricks or stones if they move through the seasons. From an environmental perspective, cement requires a greater amount of energy to be consumed during its manufacture than lime. In addition, bricks or stones that are laid in lime mortar are reusable since it is fairly easy to remove the softer lime mortar that surrounds them. Where cement has been used in the mortar mix it is usually quite difficult to remove the mortar from around the bricks without breaking them, which makes it almost impossible to recycle the bricks except as hardcore.

Damp and Decay

Decay is caused by water getting into materials that should be kept dry. Victorian and Edwardian builders were well aware of this fact and made sure that there were adequate ventilation paths through the structure of the house to allow damp to dry out. A good example of how this was dealt with is in

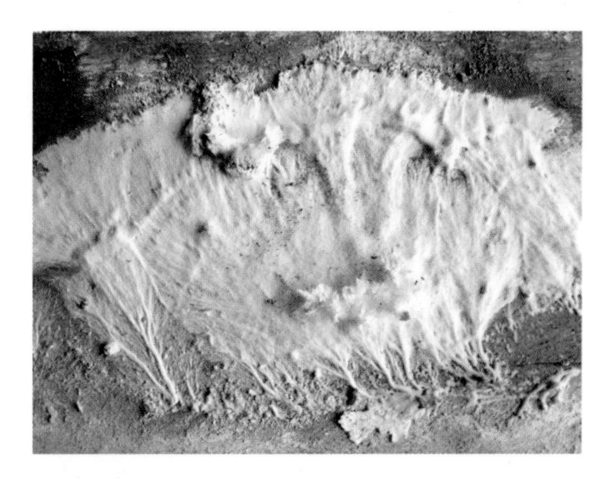

If water is allowed to get into the fabric of the house and is then unable to escape, then rots like this may become established.

Make sure that existing air vents are kept free of vegetation to allow air to circulate into the voids below timber ground floors.

This blocked air vent means that air is not circulating around the timber floor joists that are adjacent to this outside wall and may then contribute to the timber floor starting to decay.

connection with timber ground floors. Air bricks are usually found in the outer walls around the perimeter of the house, just below the level of the floor joists. These allow air to circulate throughout the underfloor spaces to keep them dry. This is why it is important that these vents are kept clear of debris. Where ventilation paths become blocked and water is retained within the fabric there are two phases that decay may go through, depending on the amount of damp. When the level of dampness increases above about a 15 per cent moisture content in timber this may attract wood-boring beetles; and when the level increases above about 20 per cent then this may encourage rot.

But there are a number of ways in which damp and decay may be reduced in and around a house. The most important precaution is to try and reduce the amount of water getting into the house because

Decorative brick air vents were often used as features so ensure that they are not blocked nor covered.

This is a decorative, cast-iron air vent placed at high level to ventilate an upper floor.

of a lack of maintenance. This may mean such things as roof or gutter leaks being mended, then areas where damp may be retained within the house should be addressed, such as earth being built up around external walls. Areas of hard paving that do not allow moisture in the surrounding soil to evaporate may also be causing problems. The ideal solution is to use water-vapour-permeable surfaces, such as gravel, that will allow water to evaporate away from the house. Where a damp problem is particularly noticeable then adding a 'French drain' around the perimeter of the house may be another possibility; this is a trench dug around the base of the house to a maximum of a little less than the depth of the existing foundations. This can then be filled with gravel level to the surrounding surfaces. But introducing as much through-ventilation as possible into the house is the best way of keeping damp levels low.

Air vents are often located under thresholds, as well as around the perimeter of the house, so check that these are clear from leaves and any other build up of materials. Preferably this should be done in spring and after the leaves have fallen in autumn. Where air vents appear to be missing check by looking at similar types of house to see whether they may have been blocked up or removed. Where ventilation paths have been previously and wrongly blocked up make sure that new ventilation holes are introduced to allow air to circulate in underfloor spaces and cellars. This is so that the timber floor structure remains dry and does not become vulnerable to damp and consequently decay.

Damp-proof Courses (dpcs)

Since many houses of this age may have slate damp-proof courses, there may sometimes be no need for an injected damp-proof course. Often the reason that injected damp-proof courses were inserted later was that the existence of an original slate course may not have been appreciated or because damp from other sources, such as condensation or the sealing-up of walls by the use of impermeable paints, was misdiagnosed. Where one does exist there might be no need for a dpc to be inserted as well. If there is damp within a house, it is usually often as a result of something else being out of balance. For example, a build up of earth bridging the damp-proof course or a change in the ground surface immediately adjacent to the walls that is preventing any trapped moisture from escaping.

Ventilation holes in the exterior brickwork provide a through flow of air to the underside of the timbers for the ground floor, otherwise the floor boards, floor joists and vertical struts that support the floor may start to rot.

Dampness in Masonry Walls

Where an impervious paint finish has been applied to either side of the wall, like a modern masonry paint on the exterior or an emulsion paint on the interior, this may seal in dampness. In time, bubbles and lumps may start to appear under the paint or plaster finish. Where damp is trapped within a solid wall it may also encourage decay to become established in any timbers that are embedded in these walls, such as floor joists or timber lintels. As with all damp problems, the most important thing is to establish what is causing them and to deal with it. Problems can range from water leaking from defective roof coverings to blocked or defective gutters and downpipes, to earth piled up against external walls. Where there is a solid internal floor, then the dampness may be a result of moisture rising up in the walls that is unable to

This shows two original layers of slate used as a damp-proof course. The green plastic plug above the slates indicates that the wall has had an injected damp-proof course added later above the original one and thus duplicates it.

Here is an example of a later injected damp-proof course (the row of plugs). If there was a damp problem, this is equally likely to have been caused by the render having covered or bridged any original damp-proof course.

The slate damp-proof course is at the same level as the external pavement, which has built up over time whereas the damp-proof course should ideally be 150mm above the external ground level to allow moisture to escape and to avoid rainwater splashing up above the level of the damp-proof course.

Laying gravel next to a wall allows water to escape from the base of the wall, even where the damp-proof course is too close to ground level, since gravel helps to reduce the amount of water splashing up the side of the wall.

evaporate from under a solid, internal, ground floor. In these situations the wall finish has to be breathable to allow any damp trapped within the wall to evaporate into the room. This damp air then has to be allowed to escape from the house, and this is where ventilation comes in.

Ventilation

Ventilation is probably the most important feature to introduce into a house to take away any dampness before it gets into the structure of the house and leads to decay. Rooms such as kitchens and bathrooms usually require additional ventilation; this is because the steam frequently in these rooms may lead to moulds and condensation if it is not properly managed by removing damp air from the house. The easiest way of doing this is by opening the window to allow it to escape. Otherwise a mechanical extractor may be appropriate. The installation of extractor fans has to be carefully considered as they can have a considerable visual impact on the exterior of the house, if they are not sensitively located. Where a house is listed permission may be necessary. It is a sensible, long-term precaution to reduce any build up of moisture in the fabric by making sure that the house has general background ventilation. The amount of background ventilation can be increased during the summer months, by, for example, opening fireplace flues (*see* Chapter 4). Any gaps around the edges of windows or doors may also benefit the general ventilation of the house during summer. In winter temporary measures that can be removed during the summer (*see* Chapter 7) may be put in place to reduce heat loss from these gaps. Another place where ventilation is important is the roof space (*see* Chapter 3) as the timbers of the roof need to be kept dry to avoid rot becoming established.

The balance between ventilation and heat conservation is a sensitive one. For example, when a fireplace that is generally used through the winter months is not alight it is prudent to cover the flue opening, so that heat generated in other ways within the house does not escape. However, where a gas fire has been installed, this requires a permanent fresh air vent in the room that cannot be closed in order to avoid suffocation.

Condensation

Condensation occurs where there is a build up of moisture within a particular room that is unable to escape; mould may start to grow as a result of warm, damp air depositing its moisture on cold surfaces. The most effective way to deal with condensation is to ensure that windows are opened to allow the moist

An impervious wall covering coupled with water from above and a lack of ventilation create the right environment for moulds to grow.

air to escape. To avoid a conflict between the disposing of stale, warm, damp air and energy conservation it is possible to use extractors that recycle the heat from waste air.

Earth Levels

Flower beds adjacent to house walls may often become built up over time and this can lead to the soil creating a bridge across the damp-proof course, so that moisture passes into the upper part of the wall, which is meant to be kept dry. Where this has happened try to reduce the height of the soil, but the drying out process may take several months, depending on the time of year. In addition, avoid planting any large shrubs close to the house since over time their roots may start to affect the foundations of the house. Another problem may arise where a rendered surface is applied over an existing brick or stone wall: the render often bridges or covers the existing damp-proof course, rather than being stopped just above it. Where this has happened, the render may be cut back to above the level of the damp-proof course to try to resolve the problem. The area of brick or stone below the damp course is intended to be able to breathe, to allow any moisture within the fabric of the house to dry out rather than being transferred to the drier wall above the damp course.

Impervious Finishes

Existing impervious finishes, such as masonry paint or cement-rich renders, have often been applied to older houses and reduce the amount of damp that is able to escape from the house. In addition, impervious paving may have been laid adjacent to a wall, so that it becomes a trap for dampness. The result is that any water that is trapped in the brick or stonework is usually unable to evaporate from the wall and the masonry may crumble and deteriorate as a result. Where there are timbers embedded in the wall or adjacent to them they too may become damp, which may encourage wood-boring beetles or rot to become established. The solution is to introduce as much ventilation or breathability into the fabric of the house as possible. This may mean that impervious finishes may need to be replaced with other types of finish (*see* Chapter 3).

Wood-boring Beetles

These are usually attracted to timbers only when they become damp, and this usually means where the moisture content rises above about 15 per cent. If sufficient air is allowed to circulate around damp timbers to allow them to dry, the beetles should, in time, disappear. There are many such beetles, but two types are particularly common in the British Isles. The usual way of distinguishing them is by the size of the flight hole that they leave in the timber. Furniture beetle or 'woodworm' holes are often about 1–2mm in diameter, whereas death-watch beetle holes are slightly larger at about 3mm. Furniture beetles are more likely to be found in Victorian and Edwardian houses as death-watch beetles are usually attracted to hardwoods, such as oak, that was less commonly used for structural timber during this period. Death-watch beetles tend to be active outside the wood only during the spring and early summer, while furniture beetles may be found for a slightly longer period. Death-watch beetles may be heard rather than seen as they alert others to their presence by tapping the wood about four or five times in quick succession. If steely blue beetles (that have a blue sheen to their bodies) are also found, this may indicate the presence of death-watch beetles, as the former are natural predators of death-watch beetles.

Where flight holes are found do not assume that they are in current use as the wood-boring beetles

Signs of woodworm are usually most visible in the spring, when deposits of fine sawdust may be found.

This is a death-watch beetle, which will usually be about 6 to 9mm long; while it may appear lifeless when found, it may jump back into action when not being watched.

A close-up of a death-watch beetle on oak (one of the favourite foods of its larval stage).

may have been extinct for a number of years. The best way to check if furniture beetles are still active is to clear away any deposits of the fine sawdust they create and wait to see if any new deposits form. As spiders are also natural predators, leaving their cobwebs in place during the spring and into the summer, which is the time when these beetles fly, is likely to be a prudent and environmentally friendly way of reducing their numbers. Because they do most of their damage in the larval stage while burrowing in wood, they can be safe from sprayed insecticides, while their predators are likely to be killed by the spray. This is why such sprays have been questioned on effectiveness as well as environmental grounds and other methods are being devised to discourage these pests. The most basic treatment is to gently reduce the dampness in the timber so that it eventually becomes unattractive to the beetles.

Rot

Where the moisture content of timber rises above about 20 per cent rot is likely to start. It results from damp conditions, so introduce as much through ventilation as possible so that the moisture content of the affected timbers is reduced. It may take several months for even superficial damp to dry out, depending on the time of year. When the timbers have had time to dry the effects of the damage may be assessed. Floor boards may need to be strengthened where they are structurally damaged. More substantial structural members will need careful examination to see whether their structural stability has been impaired. Depending on the damage, repairs might be possible by splicing in new timber to the affected areas, which is often preferable to

In nature, rotting is a natural progression when a tree dies, but to allow timbers within a house to remain damp may encourage decay to become established.

Rots and wood-boring beetles are natural in the forest as moisture levels are higher there than they should be in a house.

Rotting only thrives where there is a water supply, so by repairing the roof leaks in this situation should ensure that the rots wither and die.

complete renewal. In addition, it is likely that a higher quality and better seasoned timber may have been used when the house was built than is currently available. While dry rot is feared, it is similar to wet rot in that both types are likely to die if they do not have a food source, which is moisture-laden wood. So ensure that all areas are allowed to dry out naturally and this may deal with the rot in the process. However, be aware that fungal spores are always in the air and rot may return if ever the moisture content is allowed to increase, which means that careful attention should be paid to the regular maintenance of rainwater goods and that a build up of damp is not allowed to recur.

This rot was caused by lack of ventilation as the damp from the wall was transferred to the adjoining timber, rather than being taken away by natural ventilation.

Lime

There are a number of similar sounding terms associated with lime, but the most popular form of it is non-hydraulic 'lime putty'. This is produced when quarried limestone (calcium carbonate), burnt at a high temperature to form quicklime (calcium oxide) is then 'slaked' with water. The resulting mixture is lime putty, which looks like thick yoghurt. Slaking quicklime with less water makes hydrated lime (calcium hydroxide) which is a fine white powder. Bags of hydrated lime are usually available from most builders' merchants. This 'bag' lime is susceptible to poor storage conditions, but otherwise, if mixed with water and left in an airtight container for several months, this soon resembles lime putty. But, as with rehydrating milk from the powder form, there are slight differences between the two varieties. All lime is highly caustic until it is dry or set and can burn the skin and eyes. Great care is needed when using it and particularly when mixing it since some of the chemical reactions with water can be hot and violent. However, once it has set, dry lime is basically the same as chalk or limestone (*see* websites).

Lath and Plaster Ceilings and Walls

Generally, Victorian and Edwardian ceilings and walls, such as timber frame, were finished with a lime plaster applied over a background of timber laths. Laths are made from lengths of thin, split or sawn timber, usually about 25mm wide, and were nailed to the underside of the timber joists of the floor above or to the timber studs of wall partitions. Spaces of about the same depth as the laths (about 5mm) were then left between each piece of lathing.

A general guide to plaster mixes is that roughly three parts of sand to one of lime were used for the first coat. It usually had hair added to the mix to give it reinforcement and strength in tension. This was necessary because the timber laths may flex over the seasons. When this first coat of plaster was pressed over the ceiling laths some of it would push through the spaces between the laths to form a 'key' or 'hook' over them. This would secure the plaster in place once it had set. A second coat, again of lime and sand

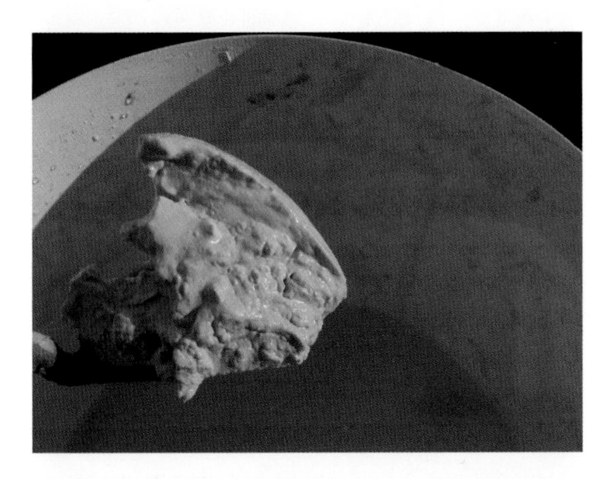

Lime putty, also known as non-hydraulic lime, is usually mixed with about three parts of sand to form lime mortars, plasters and renders (external plasters).

Certain types of animal hair may be carefully teased out into a mix of lime and sand to be used as reinforcement, but should be added to the mix only just before use, otherwise in time the wet lime is likely to dissolve the hair.

Hydrated and hydraulic limes are both supplied in powder form, so it may be difficult to distinguish between them. Hydrated lime (non-hydraulic) is used for making lime putty (non-hydraulic), as shown above, by carefully adding water to it and preferably leaving it for several months in an air-tight container. After that it can be mixed with about three parts of sand, and again kept in an airtight container, until it is used as a mortar, plaster or render. Hydraulic lime is another type of lime that may set to a greater strength than non-hydraulic lime but cannot be stored mixed as it begins to set as soon as it is mixed. The ability to set to a higher strength may not be beneficial to older houses in some situations, but it may be more useful in exposed locations on a house, as when chimneys are being re-pointed. Natural hydraulic lime (NHL) comes in three grades, from weakest to strongest, being designated NHK 2, 3.5 and 5.

Bundles of new timber laths ready for fixing to either ceilings or walls.

Laths are fixed to the background surface to which the lime mortar is applied.

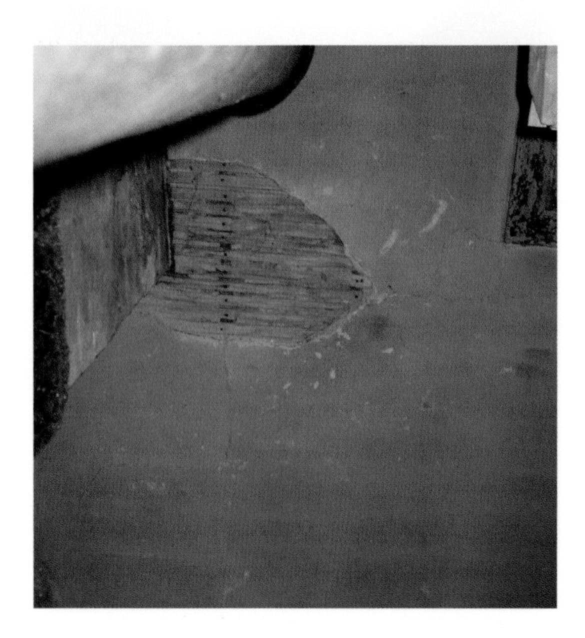

An area of exposed laths is visible, where the key (or fixing) for the plaster has been lost and the plaster has fallen away, possibly due to a roof leak. This ceiling has not been distempered for a long time so the impression of the laths and ceiling joists above may be seen on it.

The back of this lath and plaster wall shows how the first coat of plaster is pushed between the laths to form a hook or 'key' over the laths that secures the wet plaster in place once it has dried.

Patterns like these on ceiling joists or timber wall studs indicate that a lath and plaster ceiling or wall has previously been removed.

but that might not contain hair, was then applied once the first had set. The third and final or topcoat was usually much thinner in texture, may have been lime-rich and used a finer sand to achieve a much smoother finish to the ceiling. Sometimes other materials such as plaster of Paris were added to the final coat to create a crisper finish. This final coat of plaster, when dry, would then be painted with distemper.

Limewash and Distempers
Diluting lime putty with water until its consistency becomes as liquid as a conventional paint creates limewash, which is traditionally used on the exterior of houses and also often in outbuildings. Powder or natural earth pigments were often mixed with it to enhance the colour. Distemper is similar to limewash in that it is breathable, although it is made from chalk. It is usually used only internally and generally on ceilings as it does have a tendency to brush off on to clothes, which is why other types of distemper were developed with an oil binder (hence known as oil-bound distempers). The benefit of the oil is that these distempers when used on walls do not brush off on to clothing; however, their drawback is that they are not as breathable as pure distemper. Another and similar product often used in pantries and associated areas is whiting which is made from chalk, often sold in a powder form and then mixed with water. It too may be coloured with pigments.

Cement

During this period the use of cement in mortar mixes gradually gained in popularity because it meant that construction could be carried out during the winter months. This contrasts with lime-based mortar mixes that could be subject to frost damage if they were not properly set before the winter months. The disadvantage of using cement is that it is a relatively inflexible and impervious material. This means that, if the surrounding bricks or stones move a little, as they usually do with thermal expansion and contraction between the summer and winter, then there is the possibility that the inflexible mortar may start to crack. This could allow water into the brick or stonework behind. The long-term effect might be that damp became trapped in the wall, is unable to evaporate through the mortar and causes the decay of the surrounding bricks or stone. Lime-based mortars are more flexible and breathable by comparison. As cement was a relatively new product during this period its disadvantages may not then have been fully understood. It is only subsequently that the relative strengths and weaknesses of using lime and cement in old buildings have been better understood.

Paints

Originally, houses were decorated with paints that were mixed up and tinted at the house, and it is only with later developments in paint technology that ready-made paints became available. Traditional paints were tolerant of movement as well as being breathable, which allowed the fabric and structure to move and breathe. This meant that water did not become trapped within the fabric – trapped water leads to decay. Where modern paints have been applied to timber and previously painted walls, establishing what type of paint has been used is important, because many of the more common modern paints are less able to cope with movement and are not breathable. Ideally, paints have to be flexible so that the paint film does not split when the underlying surface moves very slightly. If modern paints have been used and cannot reasonably be removed, a compromise is to keep those painted surfaces in good condition and free of crack and splits so that water is unable to get in, since if it does it could be trapped by the paint. In exceptional circumstances where an impervious paint finish is clearly causing long-term damp problems, then it may be appropriate to consider carefully removing layers of less breathable paints.

This is original lead paint.

Paints for External Joinery

Traditionally, lead-based paints were used on most timber as they had the advantages of relative breathability and flexibility. This meant that water was less able to get in behind the paint and start to rot the timber. Later developments in technology created the modern gloss paints that are usually oil-alkyd based and have impervious qualities. The problem with these types is that they tend to split when the underlying timber expands and contracts. If external joinery is not regularly repainted, cracks or splits begin to develop and allow water to enter. More recently developed paints include vapour-permeable and microporous types that have similar qualities to the older lead paints, which are now no longer in general use. Another type of product that is now currently available is linseed oil paint that is probably the closest to lead-based paint. The drawback with linseed oil paints is that some manufacturers recommend that any earlier layers of paint have to be removed before their application. This destroys the history of the house in the process. Almost all old doors and windows are likely to have layers of lead paint somewhere under layers of more modern ones. Care has to be taken where lead paint is disturbed as the dust particles from dry sanding are a health concern. Also the accidental touching of lead-based paints and the inadvertent ingestion of them is also a concern. The use of blowlamps should be avoided due to the fire and health risks connected with the fumes from lead paints (*see* websites).

Paints for External Walls

Perhaps the most breathable of paints for external walls is limewash, which has been popular for centuries. Limewash is made by carefully diluting lime putty (*see* above) with water. During the twentieth century, factory-produced alternatives to limewash were developed, of which the most common nowadays is 'plastic' masonry paint. These types of paint do not allow the underlying fabric to breathe as well as limewash, so that any moisture that gets into the fabric is trapped. Impervious paints cannot be made usefully breathable except by stripping and replacing them with limewash or another highly-breathable paint; however, some of the problems of plastic masonry paint may be minimized by keeping the surface as crack-free as possible to avoid rainwater from getting under the paint finish (*see* Chapter 3).

Paints for External Metalwork

Metal railings start to rust when the paint film is punctured and water gets behind the finish and is trapped by the surrounding paint. The weakest points are junctions, either between parts of the design or the railing fixing points. Where railings are fixed into plinths the holes were originally lined with lead to create a waterproof junction. Where rust gets established at such junctions the railings may split the plinth and cause further damage. The best form of maintenance is to keep the paint film intact. Where any rust becomes apparent it should be removed to expose the bare metal. Lead paints may have been used on railings in the past and these require special precautions when they are being prepared for redecoration (*see* websites). Repainting should be carried out on a regular basis with dedicated metal primers and perhaps protective layers of micaceous iron oxide (MIO) paint, which can then be painted with a decorative coat of paint, if desired. As MIO paints tend to be quite thick they may obscure any fine details in the metalwork, so this has to be balanced against the protection of the railings for the future.

Paints for Internal Joinery

Various traditional and modern oil-based paints are likely to have been used on the woodwork in the past and, in recent years, acrylic and vinyl paints may also have been applied. Their removal should generally be considered only where they are causing a problem. Natural oil paints are now available that can allow for some breathability. As for external paints, the presence of lead in older layers of paint can potentially be hazardous (*see* websites).

The pattern of paint cracks on this timber boarding indicates that this may be a later type of lead paint, closer to modern gloss.

Paints for Internal Ceilings and Walls

When considering the redecoration of ceilings and walls, try to establish what types of paint have already been used. Where ceilings or walls have not been decorated for a number of years they may have been painted with an older, relatively breathable, non-plastic emulsion paint. Alternatively, distemper may have been used, although this is an increasingly rare survival. Distemper usually has a slightly powdery touch since it is a chalk-based paint. It is usually breathable provided that oil has not been added to the paint since this makes it slightly less breathable. The reason that oils were often added was to make it a little more resistant to wear. If any distemper remains on the ceilings or walls, consider using this breathable paint again as there are subtle variations in its texture and the way in which it reflects light that an emulsion paint, due to its uniformity, is unable to match. Other similarly breathable paints that may be found around the house are limewash (made by diluting lime putty with water) or whiting (made from chalk). Both these types of paint also have a powdery finish like distemper that enhances the quality of reflected light. These traditional types were tinted with natural earth or powder pigments to achieve the desired colour in each room. The majority of walls will now have usually been redecorated by using emulsion paints. Where modern emulsion paints have been applied these are usually not very breathable, because of the plastic-based materials in them. Where this has happened, it is sensible to use the most breathable of emulsion paints that are currently available. Trade decorators use a slightly more breathable type of emulsion paint on newly plastered modern internal walls, which may be appropriate. Another option is to choose more environmentally friendly paints but to check the ingredients to make sure that they are breathable as well, as these two qualities do not necessarily go together. Unfortunately, a non-breathable paint cannot be made breathable by covering it with a breathable paint, but by stripping off the existing paint, which may not always be achievable.

CONSERVATION IS SUSTAINABILITY

With greater awareness that energy has to be conserved to reduce carbon emissions, retaining as much of an original house fabric as is feasible is more environmentally responsible. This is also a very sustainable approach to adopt when looking after an older house, as the energy used to make the original building materials (embodied energy) has already been consumed. By taking care of these existing materials this means that smaller amounts of new materials and energy are consumed. However, where new materials are to be introduced into an older house, such as during redecoration, they should ideally be as close as possible to the original materials to avoid problems of incompatibility.

Salvage and Recycling

There is a fine line between recycling unwanted or waste materials and using those that have been removed from other houses to their detriment. There may be exceptions, but, as a general rule, try to avoid wherever possible using salvaged items since this encourages the removal of existing features from

This pile of salvaged bricks may have come from a building that was specifically demolished because of the resale value of the bricks.

other houses or their surroundings for resale. Using new designs for any features that are missing, where it is absolutely necessary to reinstate a feature, may also help future historians to understand how a house has evolved over time. In addition, by commissioning new designs this is likely to contribute to the re-establishing of craft skills and encouraging new design ideas that use traditional techniques.

Using Traditional Materials

Where new materials have to be introduced into an older house, make sure that they are compatible with the house. This means using materials that are similar in composition to those that the house was built with. The reason for this is that modern materials often behave in different ways or have different qualities from the original ones, so that they may cause problems when the two sets are used together. Where modern building materials are introduced into an older house, these are the items that are most likely to create problems. This is because they are mainly intended for recently constructed buildings that are designed on the principle of not allowing any vapour to enter the fabric, so they do not necessarily allow for letting it out. In addition, a modern house is not expected to move at all, so that there is often little flexibility in these products. For example, traditional lath and plaster ceilings are constructed of slender timber laths to which wet plaster has been applied and allowed to set. These materials allow a degree of flexibility within the sub-structure and the actual plaster itself, so there is a degree of movement built into them. By comparison, modern plasterboard, which is a factory-made, relatively rigid material, does not allow for expansion and contraction in the same way, and may crack between the joints when it is introduced into an older house as all the movement has to be concentrated into the joints between the sheets instead of being spread across the whole surface, as with lath and plaster.

Sourcing New Materials

As our awareness of how and where the food that we eat comes from and what it contains, the same now also applies to all the materials that are introduced into an older house, so owners should actively consider 'locally grown' building materials that previous generations of builders used. Not only are architects currently having to assess the amount of energy that is used in the manufacture of new building products and their composition before specifying them, they are also having to gauge exactly how far such materials are having to be transported. In addition, consideration should also be given to the working conditions of those employed to make or produce the materials. The homeowner, when considering the introduction of new materials into their domestic environment, should also use these same criteria.

Reducing Future Waste

Where new buildings are being designed, architects are now designing out as much waste as possible. For example, where sheets of building materials are being used, the dimensions of individual pieces that are to be cut from a sheet are worked out to reduce waste to a minimum. These same principles should be applied when new materials are being introduced into an older house. This is not only to reduce the amount of energy used up in producing and transporting the materials in the first place, but it also reduces the amount of materials that may ultimately have to be disposed of.

BUYING THE RIGHT HOUSE

When searching for a house, look for one that may be lived in as it is, rather than one with the intention of altering or extending it. Having building works carried out is usually stressful and may take upwards of a year to complete. The best way to avoid additional stress and expense is to buy a house that is suitable for the occupants' needs for at least the next ten years, if not longer. This approach would also benefit the house as it would not be altered and thereby lose some of its history and character in the process. After buying a house a good approach is to live in it for up to a year before considering whether any alterations are actually necessary. During this period ideas may develop or change as to what is important. It is much easier to adapt lifestyles to suit an existing house rather than to go through the complicated process of altering or extending it. Living with the house as it was originally built also benefits the house and the environment since more of the original fabric of the house and consequently its character are retained for future generations to appreciate. In addition,

New, handmade bricks are readily available in a range of colours, depending on the type of clay that was used in their manufacture. Handmade bricks may sometimes be identified by a curved line along their sides that indicates where the clay was thrown into the brick mould.

When viewing houses make sure that all aspects of them are considered before deciding to buy a particular one.

fewer new building materials will be consumed as well as enabling considerable financial savings to be made.

IDENTIFYING URGENT REPAIRS

When buying a house there are often a few repairs that may need to be attended to as a first priority. These are usually highlighted in a house purchase survey, which may be commissioned by the buyer at the time of purchase. This survey is in addition to information that is included within the Home Information Pack (HIP), called a Purchaser's Information Pack (PIP) in Scotland. These packs also include an Energy Performance Certificate, which gives an indication of the potential energy consumption of the house (*see* websites and Chapter 7).

Any urgent repairs are likely to be highlighted in a house purchase survey, but make sure that, when commissioning such a survey, the surveyor is accustomed to working on older houses. This is because such a surveyor will understand how they function, whereas one who is not so familiar with them may highlight things that are not actually problematic. Usually it is cost-effective to spend some time doing research to find a surveyor who is appropriately qualified and knowledgeable about older houses since this may save both time and money in the long term (*see* websites).

When prioritizing repairs the most important ones to start with include any water leaks into the fabric of the house; these may range from holes in the roof covering that are letting water in, to defects in the rainwater disposal system. All gutters should be cleared out and checked to see that they drain to the downpipes and that gutter joints are not dripping. If using a ladder first make sure that it is at a safe angle, securely tied and anchored, use footwear that grips the rungs well and avoid carrying heavy loads up ladders or overreaching yourself (*see* websites). In addition to the gutters, the downpipes themselves should be checked, especially on the rear face nearest to the wall to ensure that they have not rusted through and are allowing water to get into the fabric of the house. Then check that gullies at ground level are not blocked nor stopping water from being drained away from the house.

Unfortunately, the best time to look for such defects is when it is raining and preferably in heavy rain, which is when gutters are most likely to overflow. Damp may also be able to get into the house at low level through the walls if soil is banked up against them. Look to see whether there is a horizontal slate damp-proof course, which should be about 150mm above the exterior ground level. If the slate itself is not visible, then look for a slightly thicker joint between the courses of bricks at low level, as this is likely to be where a damp course may be located. Try to make sure that soil or vegetation does not cover or bridge any existing damp course. Desirably the exterior ground level should be at least 150mm below the internal floor level to ensure that damp is not able to get into the fabric of the house. Where it is possible, consider digging a shallow trench between the house wall and the adjoining soil or paths and fill it with gravel (a French drain). This is likely to allow any dampness in the subsoil to evaporate through the gravel, rather be drawn up into the fabric of the house.

By dealing with the causes of damp the amount of it getting into the fabric of the house will be lessened, but in order to dry out any existing damp, plenty of through ventilation first needs to be introduced. This means keeping windows or doors open slightly during the day where possible and opening up any blocked chimney flues to allow air to circulate. In winter, lighting a fire, if the chimney and hearth are in a suitable condition, is likely to help to dry out the brickwork surrounding the flue and generally reduce the level of damp within the house. Where a cupboard smells damp, for example, keep the door slightly open to allow air to circulate within it. This drying out process may take at least six months or more depending on the severity of the problem. Houses should be allowed to dry out naturally rather than by artificially accelerating the process. Only once a house is thoroughly dry is it sensible to consider carrying out any repairs or redecoration. These should ideally be carried out by using only breathable materials over breathable surfaces, so that even if more damp gets into the fabric in the future, which is probable, it is able to dry out much more easily next time.

Longer Term Planning for Repairs and Maintenance

The urgent repairs having been attended to, this marks only the start of an on-going process of continual, planned maintenance. The best way to approach this is to make a list of actions that might become necessary within the next five to ten years. Then put a year against when each may be necessary, together with a rough estimate of the cost involved. This will give an indication of how much money should be set aside each year for specific works on the house. For example, budget on the house needing to be redecorated every five years, so that at the beginning of the fourth and the fifth year look at the house to see whether the redecorations need to be brought forward a year, or whether they can safely left for another year.

It is sensible to take a close look at the house in

If the cause of this rot had been dealt with through a regular repainting of the exterior of this sash window damp would not have been able to gain access to the timber through splits in the paint film or through damaged putty around the glass. Once water was inside the timber it was unable to evaporate; as a result, this sash is likely to require many more repairs and more money spent on it to make it sound again. When carrying out such a repair a new piece of moulded timber would need to be spliced into the bottom rail of the sash to repair it. The existing old glass would have to be carefully taken out of the sash before the repairs were carried out, so that it could be saved and put back into the original sash when it had been repaired.

both autumn and spring to see how the house is lasting, as it is much more likely to prolong its life if small pieces of maintenance are attended to when they are first seen to be necessary rather than to leave them to worsen. This can be a more cost-effective way of dealing with repairs and it also saves building materials and resources in the process. The old saying of 'a stitch in time saves nine' is appropriate to the maintenance and repair of older houses, and it is sensible to deal with matters promptly and before they become bigger and therefore more costly to deal with. Owning an old house is about planning for future maintenance rather than leaving it until there are more serious problems to deal with that are likely to be more costly and difficult to handle.

Structural Movement

Over the years it is almost inevitable that some structural movement may occur in an older house. The most important thing is to establish whether a crack is actually increasing in size or not. It may just be the result of seasonal movement and might close up again. However, if it appears to be increasing in size over a longer period, then further investigation is likely to be needed. There will probably be weak places where cracks may open up during different seasons of the year or where different forces are at work; thus the junction between the main house and a rear extension may be a weak point, as these will be buildings of different size, probably on differing foundations but joined together at this point. Where a bay window meets the main walls of the house is another potentially weak junction. This may also be because the foundations used for the bay window were not as substantial as those of the main house and so the two elements may settle or move in different ways. This is often known as differential settlement.

Where a house has previously been partially underpinned, there is the possibility that new cracks may start to appear at the point where the underpinning stops. This may be because part of the house would be able to move on its old, original foundations more freely than the part that has been

ABOVE: Both of these houses seem to have suffered from the same problem; one appears to have been fitted with tie-bars, the other is still being propped, and it would be necessary to identify correctly the cause of the problems before deciding on a course of action.

LEFT: Where defects are noticed they should be monitored over a sensible period, to see whether the movement is on-going or historic.

Bay windows were a popular architectural device during this period, but the walls that support such a window may have less substantial foundations than the adjoining house walls. In some cases, this may result in cracking between the bay and the rest of the house due to the differential settlement between the two elements.

In this example the bay window on the right has been removed, presumably for fashion reasons or perhaps because of a problem such as the differential settlement between the house and the bay window, whereas all the other windows on this elevation appear to be original.

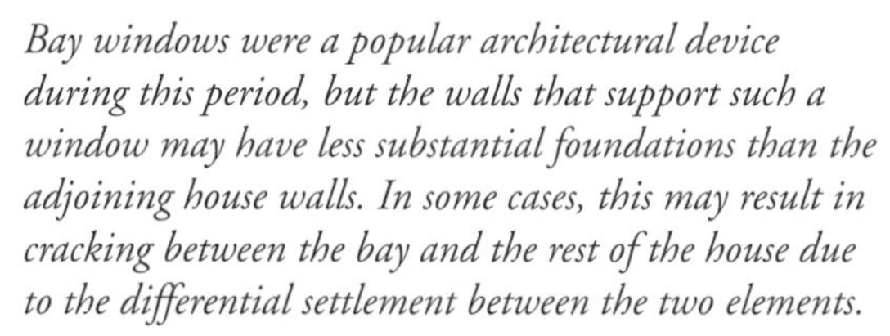

ABOVE: The settlement in the bricks above this window lintel may have happened many years earlier. Establishing whether the movement is active is essential as repairs might not even be necessary if the movement has stopped or the cause of the problem had been previously been dealt with, especially where there are no internal cracks.

RIGHT: Cracks like these are best inspected and monitored to establish whether they are simply connected with the action of the door or whether there may be other problems.

Seeing a house in this condition is unusual.

underpinned. The result might be that cracks occur at the junction between the two parts. For these reasons, underpinning is now not so popular, or is at least not always done so rigidly, since it may create more problems than it solves. Where internal walls were previously removed, they may have formed part of a load-bearing framework within the house, even if the walls that have been removed were the timber-stud partition type (*see* Chapter 4). Where a chimney breast has been removed within a room, there may be a situation where a chimney breast on a floor above or the chimney stack in the roof space may not have been sufficiently structurally supported. Where poured, often concrete-based, flue liners have been used to line an existing flue they can create a solid mass within a chimney stack that does not always allow for movement. Also, where solid floor surfaces have started to crack, if they were laid over timber floors, this may indicate that some of the support structure may have been removed from underneath the floor (*see* Chapter 4). When settlement or cracks appear to be opening up is perhaps the time at which to appoint a structural engineer with experience of working on old buildings and is accredited in building conservation to look at the problem (*see* websites) – what may appear to an engineer unfamiliar with older houses to be an expensive problem to remedy, may be considered as within acceptable tolerances for one who understands how older buildings work.

Statutory Consents for Repairs to Protected Buildings

Where a house is listed and repairs are being considered, either externally or internally, listed building consent may be necessary, depending on the extent and nature of the repairs. So, before doing anything, speak to the conservation officer in the local authority to check that any proposed repairs do not require consent. Where a house is in a conservation area and in need of repair, if it is considered that the repairs may affect its visual impact, and again depending on their nature, then consent may be necessary, but, again, speak to the local conservation officer (*see* websites).

Value Added Tax

Where a house is listed, the costs of certain specified alterations are zero-rated for VAT purposes, provided that the proposed alterations have also received listed building consent before any works had begun. Currently VAT is applicable to all repairs whether a house is listed or not. However, the definition of what is considered to be a repair or an alteration is dependent on the types of work proposed. These definitions also evolve with decisions that are arrived at through VAT tribunals. This means that where the tax is going to be a significant element of the total repairs budget where a house is listed, the advice of a tax consultant who works within the area of listed buildings might usefully be sought. Where an unlisted house has been unoccupied for a number of years there may be reduced rates of VAT applicable, but the exact criteria are subject to change over time (*see* websites). Often because of the nature of repairs to an older house, it may be more prudent to use a small builder for such works; in addition, they may not need to be registered to charge VAT. This is because they have to have a turnover above a certain annually pre-set government level each year before they are required to register and charge the tax.

Professional Help

The most important aspect of looking after an older house is to find professionals and builders who really understand traditional building construction techniques to help look after and repair the house. Where repairs are being considered it is sensible to approach either an architect or a surveyor initially as even for very small-scale works they may be able to give some useful initial guidance. The most important criteria is to find an architect or surveyor who really understands older houses. As well as being familiar with building techniques, an architect is trained in the aesthetics of design, while surveyors tend to be trained in the maintenance and repair of buildings as well as construction techniques, but the boundaries are often blurred between the two professions. Ideally, find an architect or surveyor who is accredited in building conservation. The Royal Institute of British Architects (RIBA) and the Royal Institution of Chartered Surveyors (RICS) both have accreditation systems for architects and surveyors who specialize in caring for old buildings (*see* websites). In addition, speak to the Conservation Officer at the local authority. An accredited architect or surveyor, once appointed, might suggest solutions that are much cheaper than if a general builder is approached. An architect or surveyor may progress the repairs from start to finish, which would include applying for any necessary permissions and then monitoring the works on site through to completion (*see* chapter 6). Where the nature of the repairs are such that the advice of other professionals is necessary, then the architect or surveyor may be able to suggest others to approach. The next most likely professional that may need to be consulted is a structural engineer, if there are problems with cracks in the existing house for example. As with architects and surveyors there is also an accreditation scheme for structural engineers who specialize in the care of older buildings (*see* websites).

Builders and Craftspeople

Although it is usually advisable to have some input from an architect or a surveyor to specify appropriate materials or the scope of the specifications for small works, where the works are of a sufficiently small nature for a builder to be approached direct, finding a suitably sympathetic one who understands how to care for older houses may be difficult. It usually requires some careful research, and a good place to start is usually with the local conservation officer. There may only be a limited number of builders in your area who are familiar with the materials and techniques that are appropriate to the long-term care and repair of older houses. Start by preparing a written list of the requirements and give this to the builder to price – ensuring that there is such a written list reduces the possibilities of any misunderstandings arising. The builder should then provide a written quotation for the works. Remember that an estimate is only a rough indication of what the works might cost, whereas a quotation is a price for carrying out specific items of work. However, if additional or unforeseen circumstances arise, these ought to be notified to the homeowner in advance and a price agreed before any additional works are carried out. VAT is applicable to all quotations, where the builder's turnover is over a government-set threshold. Be wary of those who suggest that, by paying cash, VAT may be avoided as this breaks the law. Agree on the scope and cost of the works, together with a timescale and starting date. Both parties should then sign a recognized and preferably impartial form of contract as a binding agreement (*see* websites). For further information *see* Chapter 6.

Plants and Houses

Generally, it is best to avoid growing ivy over walls as it may start to burrow into soft mortar and dislodge bricks or stones. Where ivy is already established, it may need to be trimmed up to four times a year to avoid its getting into gutters. Vegetation of any sort in gutters reduces the amount of water that is taken

Where creepers get into the gutters they can impede the flow of rainwater taken away from the fabric of a house and may obscure architectural details at the same time.

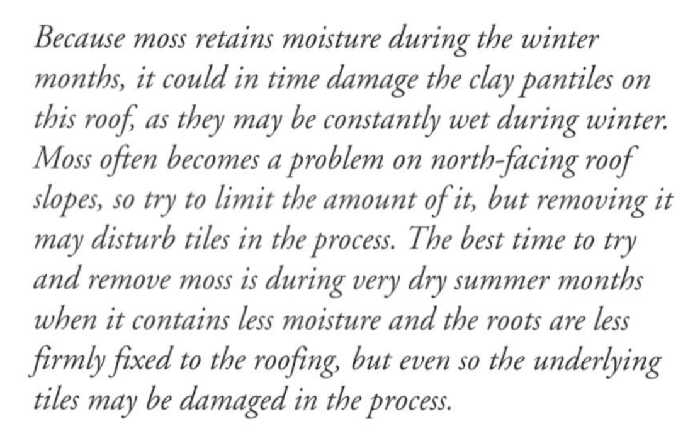

Because moss retains moisture during the winter months, it could in time damage the clay pantiles on this roof, as they may be constantly wet during winter. Moss often becomes a problem on north-facing roof slopes, so try to limit the amount of it, but removing it may disturb tiles in the process. The best time to try and remove moss is during very dry summer months when it contains less moisture and the roots are less firmly fixed to the roofing, but even so the underlying tiles may be damaged in the process.

Moss is attracted to growing on north-facing roof slopes that tend to remain wetter for longer. While it often looks attractive, the continued wetting of the underlying roof tiles may in time degrade them. Where possible try to gently remove moss during drier weather, as it is likely then to be less firmly fixed to the underlying roof.

away from the house by the rainwater disposal system. In heavy rain the gutters are likely to overflow and water is then able to start to get into the fabric of the house, creating the right conditions for damp and decay to become established. If ivy is to be removed from a wall, start at ground level by removing a section of the trunk to about 500mm in height. In addition, dig out its roots, which can often be extensive. Then leave the ivy on the wall to die naturally over a number of months. Only when the leaves are completely brown should the ivy be removed. This is because it usually attaches itself to the brick or stonework and, if removed while it is still growing, it may take a part of the wall away with it. Where a large amount of ivy has been allowed to grow over the top of garden walls, this may increase the wind resistance. During high winds, ivy may be blown off a wall or, in some cases, it may take parts of the wall with it. Where there are plants or creepers on walls this may also indicate that flowerbeds have been built up around the house. In some cases these may have bridged the slate damp course that keeps the house dry, so make sure that flowerbeds are, where possible, at least 150mm below the line of the damp course. Then prune any shrubs that have been planted close to walls to ensure that air is able to circulate between the wall and the shrubs to reduce any potential damp problems.

Wildlife

A great variety of wildlife may choose to inhabit some part of an older house – some may be welcome additions, while others may not (*see* websites).

Bats

Bats are protected and they and their roosts must not be disturbed. Before any building works are undertaken, establish whether bats are present. Contact the local authority for details of any group which may be able to carry out a bat survey (*see* websites). Bats are usually seen flying about around dusk. If they are present in a particular roof space there may be droppings apparent under the ridge boards. As their droppings are easily confused with those of mice, the only way to tell the difference is that when they are crumbled (wear protective glasses, gloves and masks

RIGHT: Bats are able to fly in and out of tiny gaps in buildings, even though their wing span appears fairly large.

FAR RIGHT: Bat droppings under a ridge board (they look similar to mouse droppings).

for this) insect remains are likely to be found since these are their staple food. Where bats are known to use an area where building works are proposed, the relevant county agency (*see* websites) has to be contacted well in advance. Where a roof covering is to be removed from a known roosting place, this has to be done before the roosting season begins, which will depend on the species but may start in early spring.

Bees and Wasps

Bees may be seen swarming in the spring and summer. A local beekeeper may be able to entice a swarm of bees away. The arrival of bees may be connected with the types of crop that are being grown locally. The homeowner may wish to have wasps' nests dealt with if they are causing a problem.

Birds' Nests

Nests are protected while in use (*see* websites) and must not be disturbed. It is a sensible precaution to use wire netting to block up any potential openings that might be attractive to birds, but without reducing useful ventilation to the house. The use of wire netting allows air to circulate within a roof space, so that any damp within or around the roof timbers is able to dry out.

Mice and Rats

Mice and rats enjoy burrowing in roof insulation, running around floor and roof voids and gnawing electric cables, so find out where they are getting into the house and block their access. Where ventilation may be compromised as a result use fine wire mesh to cover the holes.

Grey Squirrels

These enjoy burrowing in roof insulation, so try to establish how they are getting into the house and block up their entry point. Cages may be used to catch them; however, if they are caught they are classed as vermin in the United Kingdom and may not then be released.

RIGHT: Nests can have an adverse effect on decorations beneath.

FAR RIGHT: Once nests are established, as with these house martins, they are protected.

CHAPTER 3

Exterior

Looking after a Victorian or an Edwardian house is about timelessness. Imagine what someone who is seeing the house for the first time in a hundred years might see. One would hope that would be one that retained all its original features since few have been removed or altered over the intervening years. This is the most respectful way to look after an older house, so try to avoid altering how the house looks or removing its original features so that these will remain for future owners and occupants to appreciate. But where some features have already been removed this could nevertheless also be a part of the house's history and explain how it evolved over the years.

EXTERNAL COLOUR SCHEMES

As the exterior is the first part of the house to be seen on one's arrival, to make sure that it enhances rather than detracts from the house's architectural qualities is important. When thinking about colours, start by looking at the adjoining houses. For example, where a house is one of a pair or forms part of a terrace, it is likely to enhance the overall appearance of the group to paint the external features to match each other. When considering whether to reuse the existing colours or to change them some careful research is helpful before reaching any decisions. There may be clues as to earlier colour schemes where paint has

Making changes to one house may have an effect on the surrounding ones.

Colours may have an effect on how a house looks.

The sashes of this bay window are painted a different colour from that of the timber frames and so alters the visual emphasis of the house.

been chipped. Brown timber graining or darker colours may be discovered under layers of later paint. In the mid-twentieth century, doors and windows may have been painted in different colours, in contrast to those on the surrounding frames since this was a popular fashion. Metal railings and cast-iron downpipes may also have been painted in a variety of colours over the years, thus by carefully scraping away a small area of the upper layers of paint the earlier colours may be revealed.

Comparing any available old photographs of the house to the colours found may help to verify the date of a particular colour scheme. But, having chosen your preferred colours, make sure that, where appropriate, the new paints used are breathable or microporous to allow the fabric of the house to breathe (*see* Chapter 2). If you are considering a new colour scheme for a house listed or in a conservation area, consent may be necessary, so first contact the local conservation officer. In addition, be aware that older layers of paint may be lead-based and require special precautions in their preparation for redecoration (*see* websites).

The lintels over the windows remain as originally intended on the near house, while those of the bay windows further away have been painted, which changes the architectural emphasis of the elevation.

ABOVE: Fine chimneys enhance the stature of a house.

RIGHT: Chimneys may be a striking feature of a house.

CHIMNEYS

Open fires were the main source of heat until central heating became popular in the mid-twentieth century. This meant that most rooms had a fireplace and a chimney to take the smoke away. As chimneys normally form the highest point on a house, the scaffolding needed to gain access to them is usually expensive and difficult to put up without damaging the roof covering. Chimneys are usually in exposed positions, so the mortar that surrounds the bricks or stones on the chimneystack, which is known as the pointing, may deteriorate quicker than on other parts of the house. Where a chimney has previously been repaired or rebuilt it is likely that a mortar mix containing a high proportion of cement has been used.

Mortar mixes like this are less flexible and tend to crack more readily, as cement in a mortar is a relatively inflexible material. If the mortar surrounding the bricks or stones does not expand and contract at the same rate, cracks may start to appear. These then start to allow water to get into the fabric of the chimney stack. As moisture is unable to evaporate through this impervious mortar, it starts to damage the surrounding bricks or stones. Where a cement-based mortar has been used for the flaunching (the capping to the chimney top that also holds the pots in place) it may be almost impossible to remove the mortar from around the chimney pot without

This chimney has been fitted with a spark arrestor to reduce the likelihood of sparks from the flue getting into the thatch. The drawback with these circular metal cages is that they have to be regularly cleaned to avoid a build up of tar in them since this can become a fire hazard. Gaining access to these devices is usually difficult. Television aerials are also often attached to chimneys, so consider their visual implications for the setting of the house and whether they could be located in less obtrusive places.

damaging it. Chimneys usually need to be totally rebuilt only where there are significant structural problems. The cause of the original problem must be fully understood and dealt with before any rebuilding is considered. If this is the only option, then consider whether it is reasonable to reuse the existing building materials as they presumably will match the house. An alternative to the use of cement in the mortar mix is hydraulic lime since this is a more flexible and less impervious material than cement. Hydraulic lime is a little more resistant to frost during the winter months than non-hydraulic lime (Chapter 2), but seek professional advice on this as situations vary.

Where there are tall, freestanding brick chimneys there may be a case for attaching metal stays around them and tying them back to the house. Where the existing chimney pots have already been replaced, one reason could be that a flue liner has been installed, since these usually require a different type of chimney terminal. If replacement chimney pots are necessary at any point, consider the visual implications of any change since they may have a considerable effect on the appearance of the house.

Where nesting birds have become a problem it may be possible to put ventilated clay caps on unused chimney pots. Where a gas appliance is being installed the flue liner may require a different type of chimney terminal that may not blend in well with the existing pots unless it is carefully chosen. For houses in exposed locations, lightning conductors may be appropriate; the route of the metal conductor tapes has to be carefully considered as they have to run from the highest point, which is usually a chimney, down to ground level and it is desirable that they do not detract from the house's appearance, as may also television aerials and satellite dishes, often fixed to chimneys, if not carefully sited. For this reason where a house is listed or in a conservation area permissions are usually necessary (see websites).

ROOFS

The two most popular materials used for roofing during this period were slates and clay tiles. Slates were common on Victorian houses, while clay tiles became more popular on later Victorian and Edwardian houses. However, the extensive use of

An example of a 'butterfly' roof, where the slope is to a central valley.

slate became possible only once the railway network had been developed. The most noted area for slate quarries was North Wales, where slates are still being produced. Clay tiles were often made at the local brickworks rather than being transported greater distances. The most expensive roof covering was likely to be used on the main house, and, where the finances allowed, this same material was also used on the rear extension. However, where there were locally produced materials readily available, these may have been used on less visible roofs. Where the roof is concealed behind a parapet wall the house may have a 'butterfly' roof – this has a central drainage or 'valley' gutter that slopes from the front to the back of the house, with a downpipe on the rear elevation. These roofs are usually covered with slates as they are more suitable for laying at lower pitches than clay tiles.

Ridge and Hip Tiles

Ridge and hip tiles were used to weatherproof the angled junctions between roofs. Decorative ridge tiles were popular on slate and clay roofs. Gable ends may have been further embellished with decorative finials. Stone roofs generally have ridge tiles carved from single pieces of stone. In some areas clay may be used instead for the ridge tiles. Many original ridge and finial tiles still survive and, where a roof is to be relaid, these should be reused. The difficultly in trying to reuse existing ridge, hip and finial tiles is that they may have previously been attached by using cement mortar; the problem is that these tiles may be broken when one tries to remove the cement-based mortar from them. Obtaining new replacements that are a close or suitable match may be difficult, so great

These decorative ridge tiles and finials at the ends of the gables enhance the architectural detailing of this house which is covered in clay tiles.

The middle roof has lost its decorative ridge tiles while others still keep theirs.

care has to be taken when handling these tiles to avoid breakages. Where ridge tiles have already been removed and replacements are being considered, make sure that any new tiles are appropriate, rather than too decorative or too plain for a particular type of house.

Slate Roofs

Slates from the Welsh quarries were generally the most commonly available and these tend to have a greyish colour. As these slates were easier to split and shape than other types, they tended to be laid in regular courses. Slates from other parts of the country were laid in diminishing courses, where the smallest slates were used on the top row and increased in size towards the base of the roof. This technique was adopted to make the most use of the different sizes of slate available. There are several ways of fixing slates: they can either be nailed into horizontal timber roofing battens that are in turn fixed on to the roof rafters, or they can be fixed direct on to 'sarking' boards (butt-jointed timber boards laid across the

Slate was the most popular type of roof covering once the railway network allowed them to be transported far greater distances from the quarries.

rafters); sometimes battens were also fixed to sarking boards.

Slate is a highly durable material, but the weak point in its use is usually the nails used to fix the slates to the timber battens – over time these may corrode and then the slates may slip, this is commonly known as 'nail sickness'. Another potential weakness is the corrosion of the nails used to attach the battens to the rafters. Over time, the battens may begin to sag and, consequently, the slates start to slip. In certain conditions the slates may also start to delaminate and this is usually more pronounced on north-facing roofs, where the sun is unable to dry them out regularly.

A slate roof may last for about a hundred years before it has to be repaired. When one is to be relaid, ensure that as many as possible of the existing slates are reused, as they are a diminishing natural resource. For example, in Scotland there are currently no quarries producing the distinctive local slates, so to find a close match with new slates is time-consuming and costly, compared with the reuse of the existing slates. Where larger slates have been damaged because the original nail holes have grown larger, these might be reduced in size and then reused. This involves knapping in which the edges of the slates are chipped to form a straight line. Where there are not enough existing slates to reuse on one particular roof slope, try to use the older ones on areas where they will be visible, as their colour will have weathered over the years. Choose new slates to match the existing ones as closely as possible. Where a roof is being relaid this can be an appropriate time to introduce a breathable roofing membrane underneath the slates (see later in this chapter). But before any works are proposed check that bats are not present in the roof space (*see* Chapter 2).

Clay Tiles

During the Victorian period clay tiles evolved from flat ones to ones with nibs modelled into the top of each and, as the use of machine-made tiles developed, they became more regular and smoother than hand-made tiles. They were able to be hung over timber battens without nails, but as an additional precaution, some, if not all of the rows of tiles were nailed into battens for additional fixings. The weakest point

These green slates are from Cumbria and are usually laid in diminishing courses to make the most use of the different sizes of slate available.

The lighter coloured dots on this slate roof are 'tingles', used to keep slipped slates in place. Tingles are J-shaped metal strips; one end is nailed on to the horizontal timber batten, the other end is folded up over the lower edge of the slipped slate to keep it back in its position. Tingles provide a holding repair until the whole roof is ready to be relaid using as many of the existing, sound slates as possible.

Where tiles have been damaged they must be repaired to stop water entering the roof space, which may lead to rot beginning. But try to use tiles that are similar to the existing ones so that the repair patches are less visible.

with these 'nibless' tiles can be the metal fixings. If these start to corrode then each row, with all the weight of the tiles on it, starts to slip down on to the next one. Water may then be able to enter the roof space, and this may contribute to wood-boring beetles or rot becoming established (*see* Chapter 2). Where the odd tile begins to slip, a new nibbed roof tile matching the existing ones, may be pushed back into position by carefully lifting up the surrounding tiles and pushing the new one over the existing batten. To get access to missing tiles is often costly, requiring scaffolding or a portable lifting platform, and, when one tile is being put back, others may be disturbed in the process.

Where a number of tiles are damaged, try to obtain new tiles that are a close match to the existing ones. There are now a great variety of new tiles available so a close match is achievable, but this usually involves some careful research. When a significant number of tiles have begun to slip, the existing ones may be carefully taken off and reused. Depending on the number involved and the degree of wear, consider positioning sound, weathered tiles on the most prominent roofs and group any new tiles that may be necessary to make up for broken or damaged ones, on hidden roofs to allow them to weather. When the roof covering is being relaid, consider adding a breathable roofing membrane underneath the tiles (*see* below). Before any works are proposed check that bats are not present in the roof space (*see* Chapter 2).

Stone Slates

The individual pieces of stone used to form a roof are rather confusingly usually known as 'stone slates'. Holes were traditionally punched or drilled into the top or 'head' of each slate, which was then hooked over a horizontal timber batten by using a timber, usually oak, peg though this hole. However, from the nineteenth century onwards, nails were used in place of timber. Where individual stone slates have slipped it may be possible to refix them by pivoting adjoining slates out of the way to gain access to the timber batten behind. Where the metal fixings have begun to fail this is an indication that the roof may eventually need to be relaid. However, great care must be taken when removing existing stone slates in order to ensure that as many as possible are saved to be used again. This is because to find new slates to match the existing ones is often difficult as many quarries ceased production once the stone became too costly to extract or the quarry's supply was exhausted.

These limestone slates are laid in diminishing courses.

Pantiles

Even medieval pantiles were of similar sizes, but there have been many variations in the design of pantiles so to find an exact match might be difficult. Where any building works are being carried out near these tiles, take great care to ensure that they are not damaged in the process. Where individual tiles have started to slip they may be carefully refixed, but be aware that many more may be damaged in the process. When a number of tiles are beginning to slip this is an indication that this is an appropriate time to consider relaying the existing tiles. Before any works are proposed check that bats are not present in the roof space (*see* Chapter 2).

A close-up detail of original pantiles; modern tiles and laying would tend to be more regular, resulting in some loss of character.

RIGHT: *The pantiles used on this rear extension are a variation of the traditional S-shaped ones found particularly along the east coast of the United Kingdom and around the Bristol area. Locally available roofing materials were often used on rear extensions where they were less visible and less expensive than the slates used on the main house roof. These local designs may be difficult to replace.*

BELOW: *Pantile replacements, such as on the left, can quickly blend with older roofs if the tiles are carefully chosen.*

Lead

Wide sheets of lead can be joined together to create flat roofs – over a flat-roofed bay window, for example. Where regular access is required over an existing lead roof, to clear out gutters or hopper heads, for example, consider laying timber duck boards, slatted boards laid over the lead to protect it from damage. Lead is also used in narrower strips to create a weatherproof joint between different materials or at junctions between the same roofing materials. As lead expands with heat, it has to be carefully fixed in place to allow for expansion and contraction to take place, because it may buckle and then crack if it is too restricted in its movement. Where lead has cracked, even only with hairline cracks, this may allow considerable amounts of water to enter the building fabric, and thus should be repaired as soon as possible. In addition to visible lead flashings, there may also be hidden ones underneath the junctions between slates or tiles called 'soakers', which are used as an added level of protection to try to prevent water getting into the fabric of the house.

Party Walls

The party walls that separate houses from one another often rise to just beneath or just above the roofs and these walls create a physical separation between adjoining properties. However, in many terraces where a party wall is not visible above the roof, this may mean that this wall has been built only up to the height of the bedroom ceilings. Consequently the roof spaces of adjoining properties might be interconnected. With a greater awareness of fire safety, security and sound transmission, purchase survey reports often highlight that party walls should now be built up to the underside of the roof covering in order to reduce these risks.

Concrete Tiles

Concrete roof tiles have often been used as replacements for slate- and clay-tiled roofs in the recent past. Where they have already been used, consider using a closer match to the original roof covering when reroofing becomes necessary. Concrete tiles are not normally acceptable on listed houses nor those within conservation areas. Where one house in a group has been reroofed with these, it tends to distort the visual balance of the whole group.

Remedial Repair Products for Roofs

There are many products available that claim to increase the lifespan of slated or tiled roofs. Highly adhesive paints that are applied to the exterior of roof coverings are not usually removable. This means that,

Lead flashings are often used over the changes in angle of slated or tiled roofs above bay windows, and may include a timber roll under the lead to give it height and shape.

Stepped lead flashings are used to make the joint watertight between different materials, as here between a brick wall and a slate roof. The stepped flashing is pushed into the mortar joint and secured in place by lead wedges that are then covered with mortar. There will usually be a second layer of lead 'soakers' beneath the flashing, interleaved with each slate or tile.

This row of cottages may have originally been built with interconnected roof spaces, but this can only be established by looking inside them.

when the roof is relaid, the slates or tiles have to be completely replaced, which is more expensive and less environmentally friendly as more new materials have to be used. A recent remedial measure for keeping roof slates in place is spray-applied insulation installed beneath roof tiles and slates. This is sprayed over the roofing battens as well as the underside of the slates. But a problem with this method is that roof timbers and timber battens may then be encased in foam, which does not allow air to circulate around them. Moisture is then unable to escape from the timbers and this may create an appropriate environment for beetles or rot to become established. After this material has been applied to the underside of a roof, slates and tiles are less easily reused and therefore the cost of reroofing in the future is likely to be higher as a completely new roof may be necessary.

The roof on the far right has had a finish applied over the tiles, the centre two roofs have had replacement concrete tiles and the only original roof is just visible to the left of the left end gable, which adjoins another roof of concrete roof tiles.

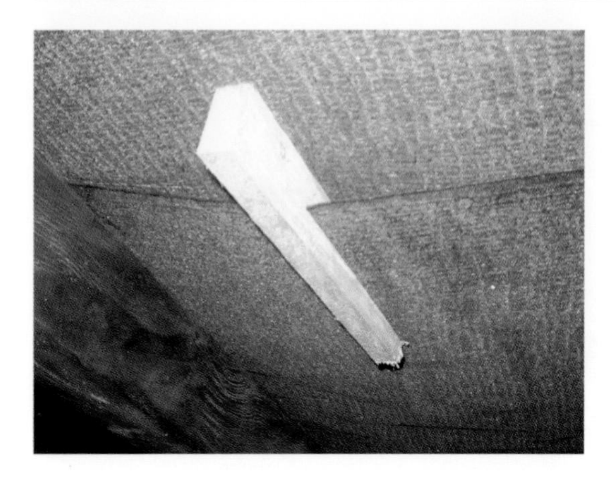

This is an example of an earlier type of underlay that is not breathable. Timber spacers have been introduced to try to increase the level of ventilation within the roof space.

Roofing Underlays

The original roof would usually have been laid without any fabric or sheet underlay being used, so the underside of the existing roofing will usually still be visible. There are, however, parts of the country where woven rush or straw was used beneath the tiles. Where a roof has already been relaid, a roofing underlay would often have been added between the roof rafters and the tiling battens as additional protection against water gaining access to the roof space. Most early types of underlay were impervious, and it is only the recently developed underlays that are more breathable. Introducing an underlay reduces the amount of ventilation through a roof space, so new ventilation paths have to be carefully designed to ensure that the roof timbers have plenty of air circulating around them. The reason that ventilation is so important in a roof space is to ensure that the moisture content in the roof timbers does not reach a high enough level for beetles to be attracted to the timbers or for rotting to begin. When a roof is being considered for reroofing, a new and highly breathable underlay, which may mean replacing an earlier type, is usually appropriate. Before any works are proposed check that bats are not present (*see* Chapter 2).

Although this is a later type of roofing felt than in the previous example, it is still an impervious type as not all modern underlays are usefully breathable, so try to find one that is.

Roof Ventilation

Where an existing roof does not have a roofing underlay between the roof structure and the existing roof covering, there is usually a sufficient flow of air though the gaps between the slates or tiles to ensure sufficient ventilation. Some roofs may have original square or 'butt'-edged timber (sarking) boards, which usually had spaces between them, so that air is able to circulate around the roof space to reduce the moisture content of the timbers. If an attic or roof space feels stuffy or too hot in summer, it is likely that there is a lack of through ventilation. In these situations the level of it would need to be increased to ensure that the moisture content in the timbers does not rise above the level at which beetles or rot may start to attack them. If insulation has been introduced into a roof space it may have inadvertently been placed over ventilation gaps resulting in a reduced airflow. The most likely problem areas are between the base of the roof structure and the walls, so ensure that these ventilation paths are clear. To reduce the amount of heat loss from the house additional layers of insulation may be laid in the roof space. In these situations try to ensure that the timbers do not become encased in insulation as this will reduce the amount of air that is able to circulate. The priority in roof ventilation is that moist air is taken away from the roof timbers and that they are kept as dry as possible.

When cast-iron downpipes are being refixed, ensure that there is sufficient space behind the pipes to allow for them to be repainted as this is the most vulnerable place for rust to become established.

This gutter has a decorative lion-head covering the joint between sections. The downpipe has been fixed into the bricks rather than into the mortar joints, which may damage the bricks in the long term.

RAINWATER DISPOSAL SYSTEMS

The most important part of the house to keep properly maintained is the rainwater disposal system. Water needs to be swiftly taken away from the house so that it does not have the opportunity to get into the fabric and feed decay. Houses of the date in which we are interested were usually originally constructed with cast-iron gutters and downpipes, and it was only in the middle of the twentieth century that plastic, or in some cases asbestos cement, started to be used as a replacement. Where cast-iron gutters and downpipes have been replaced with plastic – which has its environmental critics –

Make sure the guttering complements the house.

reinstatement with iron is preferable for its authenticity and, if properly maintained, many aspects of its performance and aesthetic qualities.

Cast-iron gutters are made watertight at the joints with a compound inserted between the overlapping ends that are then held and compressed by nut and bolt. Where these joints start to leak, they may be taken apart and filled with new jointing compound. However, this is usually a major operation that involves taking the guttering down, and it is usually sensible to do it when the gutters are being redecorated. As a temporary repair to stop water from getting into the fabric there are a number of water-resisting tapes or mastics that may be applied to the interior of the gutter, but these do not last indefinitely. Where the existing cast-iron guttering has previously been replaced with plastic gutters, they may also start to leak at the joints; this is usually due to the rubber jointing gaskets having failed. Joints may be taken apart, thoroughly cleaned and dried out before reassembly. If the original manufacturer's gaskets are no longer available a standard pattern may be tried.

Where the rainwater downpipes meet the ground there is usually an open gulley with a square metal grating over it. This is to protect the underground drainage system from becoming blocked by leaves or moss from the roof. This drainage may either lead into a soakaway, which is a drainage pit located somewhere nearby in the garden and a popular type in rural areas, or the drain may be connected into a combined system, with the soil pipe waste, that runs into the main sewerage system. This latter system is more usual in towns and is called a combined system. If there are any drainage plans with the house these may help to identify which type of system is in use, otherwise start by looking inside any manhole covers to see how many pipes enter and leave the drain and the directions in which they flow. Check the gullies around the house on a regular basis to ensure that they are running freely. The best time to do this is when it is raining particularly heavily, since any defects or blockages are likely to be most evident then. Ideally, gutters should be cleaned out at least twice a year, in spring and in autumn, just after all the leaves have fallen. This is likely to reduce the risk of water being able to find its way into the fabric of the house from any unnoticed defects in the rainwater system. Where manholes are located in the garden try to avoid placing heavy objects over them as they often need to be opened in a hurry when a problem has arisen.

Where the back of this downpipe has not been painted it is beginning to rust through.

This cast-iron downpipe is beginning to rust in places and requires redecoration before the rust becomes established. The fixing points are set within the mortar courses, so that the bricks were not damaged when the fixings were inserted.

Vegetation like this growing near a downpipe indicates that the back of the pipe may have rusted through and that water is probably getting into the fabric of the house and may cause serious problems if left unattended. The brickwork is an example of Flemish bond.

SOIL PIPES

This is the term for the large diameter, vertical pipes that are used to take wastewater away from sinks and toilets. These pipes usually have to have a vent at the top of the pipe, if there is not a separate vent that admits air to the drain. This type of plumbing was usually sited well away from the main elevation of the house. Most original plumbing pipes were made of either lead or cast iron, so avoid replacing any of these with plastic components as these are likely to transmit more sound when being used, as well as being less in keeping with the original design of the house. Often where lead pipes still exist they are a work of art in themselves, they may often have decorative designs for the brackets that fix the pipes to the walls. Where new plumbing is being considered, such as soil stacks and underground drainage for new bathrooms, try to position these on the rear elevation, rather than on the front where they can have a considerable visual impact on the setting of the house.

WALLS

Walls were usually constructed of locally available materials and this usually meant either brick or stone as these were probably the ones most readily available, but where local materials such as flint or pebbles were more economically available then these were often used in preference.

Brick

Bricks were laid in many different patterns, but one of the most popular is known as Flemish bond. The long face of a brick, a stretcher, is laid next to a header, the short end, to create a solid, bonded wall

Drains may become overwhelmed during heavy rain.

Detail of grey header bricks contrasted with the surrounding red bricks.

Contrasting bricks are used to outline the door and windows.

'Tuck' pointing is found where a narrow line of white, lime-rich mortar is used to highlight the joins between the bricks.

that is usually 9in thick as a minimum. Solid brick walls were common for external walls; but from about 1870 onwards, cavity walls started to be used that were two rows of stretchers, with a space between the two walls. These were tied together with metal wall ties. Snapped headers, where a brick has been cut in half lengthwise, may have been used to give the impression that the wall was solid rather than a cavity wall. Check the total thickness of the wall as this may give an indication of the type of construction used. Walls were usually thicker at the base than on upper floors to support the structural loads.

To embellish what might otherwise be fairly plain brickwork, many types of decorative detailing were often introduced. These could range from brick plaques to rope mouldings and decorative, patterned bricks that could be incorporated into the detailed design of a house.

This is called 'rat-trap' brickwork, where two skins of bricks are laid on their side, with the short end of a brick (the header) used to join the two walls together for stability. This is an early form of cavity brickwork but was probably used on side walls and outbuildings simply to save bricks.

This is a cavity wall dating from 1870. However, the bricks were laid to resemble a solid wall by using 'snapped' headers.

These two rows of rope designs add a pleasing detail to this house, but the repointing below them unintentionally draws attention away from their delicate design.

This brick plaque is intact even though there have been repairs to the surrounding brickwork.

This decorative brick detail is under a gutter.

ABOVE: *Decorative bricks between the windows contrast with the detailing of the artificial stone lintel below.*

LEFT: *An interesting brick arch detail which may also have included ventilation.*

Stone

Stone was used for the walls of many houses during this period where it was readily available. As a general indication, the type of stone used north of a line drawn from the Humber estuary on the east coast down to Bristol in the south-west is more likely to be sandstone, while stones south of this line are usually limestone. Granite is usual in Scotland, Cornwall and a small area of Cumbria, where it was readily available.

Stone is used for the walls and roof slates of this bay-windowed house.

Locally available building stones and slate were used for this Scottish house.

LEFT: The durability of stone depends on a number of factors, such as its quality, how it is laid in relation to how it was deposited in the quarry, and where it has been used on the building. Here the stone has been subject to wind erosion in an exposed coastal location.

BELOW: This is an example of coursed stonework, where each piece has been cut into a rectangular-shaped block before it was laid. Random stonework was used for walls where the stone was difficult to cut or 'dress' into shape or simply to save the expense of dressing it properly.

Brick and Stone Repairs and Repointing

The problems that affect brick and stone walls are often very similar. The main cause of decay is usually damp being unable to evaporate from the walls. By remaining in the walls the water causes the decay of bricks or stones. This often becomes noticeable where the faces of the bricks or stones begin to flake or spall, assisted by the action of frost. Another problem that affects walls occurs where they were originally constructed with lime-based mortars but have subsequently been repointed with a cement-based one. The introduction of an impervious material, such as cement (*see* Chapter 2), into the joints between the stones or bricks means that any water that does get into the wall is unable to dry out behind the mortar. The water then lingers in the wall and causes the bricks or stone to decay. Where stones are held in place by hidden metal cramps, any damp in the walls may start to rust the cramps and the expansion of the rust will eventually split the stone.

Repairs are arguably only appropriate where the damage is actually adversely affecting the bricks or stones. For example, where a projecting brick or stone moulding, usually known as a 'hood' moulding is damaged over the arch of a doorway it is appropriate to repair this as its purpose is to deflect water away from the doorway. However, where the doorway is already protected by, for example, an overhanging balcony, this is likely to be sufficient protection. In situations where there are missing pieces of decorative motif, provided that they do not

Cracks like these may be due to structural movement or some other reason, so make sure that the problem is fully understood before works are carried out.

The original lime mortar was not raked out sufficiently before the repointing; however, the replacement cement mortar has also failed because of its inflexibility and imperviousness.

Trowels used for repointing mortar joints.

This old brickwork has been repointed with cement mortar that is more likely to accelerate decay in the brickwork as it does not allow it to breathe or move. This style of pointing is known as 'struck' pointing, which is very angular by comparison with the surrounding brickwork.

This replacement mortar has feather edges over the existing granite which are likely to flake off when attacked by frost.

This random stone has been repointed with a 'ribbon' style of pointing that is cement-based, which might even cause more long-term damage to the stones than if it had not been done.

This stone work has been repointed with cement mortar and this might cause more damage in the future than if the old pointing had been left undisturbed.

have an effect on the weathering of elements around the house these may be left as they are.

Where an existing mortar appears to be soft or powdery to the touch this is not necessarily a defect with an old lime mortar, rather it indicates that the mortar is flexible, which to some degree can be beneficial to the house and it may be appropriate to leave it undisturbed. In situations where bricks or stones do require some repair it is usually difficult to find matching bricks or stone from the same clay bed or quarry. It might be possible to cut out and turn around damaged bricks or stones, otherwise a mortar repair may be used for small areas, by using sand and lime mixed with particles of the damaged brick or stone to achieve a matching colour. (This can work reasonably well with limestone and some soft bricks, but harder bricks and some stones may respond less well or be incompatible with this type of repair.) Pointing to brick and stone usually erodes slowly, so there is often little reason to completely renew the pointing. The areas that might be considered are small ones, where the pointing is visibly missing to a considerable depth, as repointing of the whole elevation is not usually necessary. Where this has been done, unless the mortar has been removed or 'raked out' – to about 25mm for a 10mm-wide mortar joint – any new pointing is likely to fall out within a few years as there is usually insufficient bonding or 'key' to keep the mortar wedged into the joint.

If repointing is necessary for small areas because a substantial depth of mortar is missing from the joints, then start by trying to establish what the original mortar mix was. If the existing material is

Sometimes it may be better to leave well alone. Here the pointing material does not match visually and if the material is over-hard, such as 'white cement', then it may do long-term damage to the surrounding bricks.

This repointing does not mirror the style of the surrounding pointing as little pieces of flint known as 'galletting' are now missing from the areas between the windows.

Be aware that repointing can significantly alter a wall and that it should be possible to match existing styles rather than impose a new look.

scraped with a sharp point and starts to flake away, it is likely to be lime-based. If there are white pieces of unburnt lime in the mortar this also indicates that this is a lime-based mortar. However, where the mortar can be scraped without its making much of an impression, this is likely to be cement-based. Try to establish whether this mortar is the original mortar mix or a later replacement. Look for clues such as whether the brickwork has been damaged when the original mortar was being raked out. Where angle grinders have been used to remove the existing pointing there may be marks where the grinder has cut the bricks, which is why their use should be avoided where older bricks are being repointed. A replacement mortar should match the existing original one as closely as possible, rather than any later mortars that have been used. A new lime mortar may look rather new for a few years, but it does tone down quite quickly. Where any masonry is to be repointed, a style that matches the existing one is the most appropriate. This is usually a slightly recessed, flat pointing between the stones or bricks, so that their edges are not covered by mortar. This also means that the bricks or stones have a more prominent visual emphasis than the mortar does, and setting back the mortar face is particularly useful where the corners of the bricks or stones have weathered since it avoids the mortar spreading over the face of the masonry.

In the past, damaged bricks were often 'faced-up' with a hard, cement-based mortar. To cover up a damaged brick surface in the short term may look good initially, but this is likely to store up problems for the future because the cement-rendered surface, even though it may be coloured to match the brickwork, does not expand and contract at the same rate as the surrounding brickwork. In time, it may become separated from the background brick and, as that may expand and contract at a different rate, cracks may start to appear. Water may then get in between the two materials and eventually the outer surface of the decayed brick may flake or spall off.

Cleaning Brick and Stone

Unless bricks or stones have a build up of deposits that appear to be causing decay, there is usually little justification for cleaning brick or stonework since

ABOVE: These bricks have been face-repaired with cement mortar, which in time damages more of the brick behind.

LEFT: The decay in these bricks has been accelerated by generations of impervious paving splashing rain up the wall and trapping damp; the remedial cement plinth has probably contributed to moving the problem further up the wall.

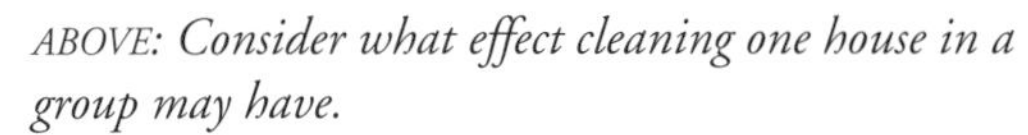

ABOVE: Consider what effect cleaning one house in a group may have.

ABOVE RIGHT: The brickwork on this house has been cleaned.

RIGHT: This similar house has not been cleaned; however, the bay windows and porch have been painted which has changed the appearance of the house.

this may lead to longer-term problems because masonry can, over time, acquire a self-hardened skin that protects itself and this could be lost. In addition, where a house forms part of a group, the balance of the harmony is likely to be distorted where one house only is cleaned. Where a house is listed or in a conservation area permission may be necessary to do this so speak to the local conservation officer.

ABOVE: The bricks on the left have been cleaned, which has highlighted white pieces of not fully slaked lime in the mortar.

LEFT: This stone inscription is on a pair of houses; that on the left has had its brickwork cleaned.

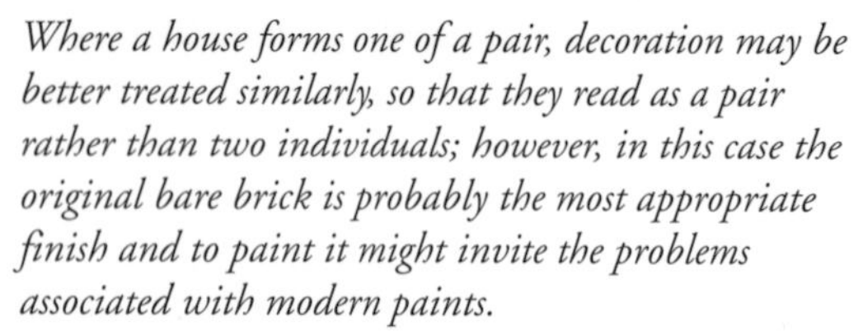

Where a house forms one of a pair, decoration may be better treated similarly, so that they read as a pair rather than two individuals; however, in this case the original bare brick is probably the most appropriate finish and to paint it might invite the problems associated with modern paints.

This bay window has recently had its paint removed. This allows the underlying surface to breathe and reduces the maintenance liability of repainting in the future. The difference between stone and artificial stone is usually noticeable by their texture as there is usually natural graining in stone, whereas artificial stone or render tends to have a more uniform appearance as the decoration was cast in a mould rather than being carved.

Paint Removal

The development of modern plastic paints has led to an enthusiasm to paint brick, stone and artificial stone features to brighten them up. Unfortunately, this type of paint does not allow the underlying surface to breathe and is not sufficiently flexible for many old buildings. Problems occur where the paint surface does not move at the same rate as the underlying masonry. This surface starts to crack and then allows water into the fabric through the paint skin, at which point the wall may start to decay. Now that the effects of sealing up walls are understood, there may be situations where removing the paint may be desirable. Many removal methods are simply too aggressive for softer, traditional building materials and will erode them, but there are now removal methods that use indirect abrasive sprays, or perhaps steam cleaning, that are more sensitive and less damaging to the underlying surface. A critical factor with any cleaning method is the sensitivity and experience of the person operating the equipment, so ensure that tests on small areas are carried out before proceeding with larger ones.

Paint is often used to cover non-matching bricks; however, a plastic-based paint finish is likely to trap damp.

When carrying out paint removal there comes a point during the process where it is prudent to stop before any unnecessary damage is done to the masonry. This may be reached before all the paint has been removed. Expect to see flecks of the former paint colour still on the walls, as there are usually areas where the paint is still well adhered and trying to remove it may cause more damage than leaving it alone.

White masonry paint has recently been removed from this brick wall but small areas still remain in defects in the original bricks. But many of the benefits of stripping the plastic paint have been lost because the wall is newly repointed in cement mortar which can also seal up the bricks.

Wall surfaces were often painted where repairs had been carried out using different bricks, since paint is a good way of disguising repairs. Where paint has been removed it may reveal an unsightly array of different bricks – each case may be different, so expect there to be yet more works necessary once the paint has been removed. Reinstating the brickwork back to its original former appearance may not be achievable, so there may be cases where the bricks have to be recovered. Where this happens, or where too many ugly flecks of old paint remain, the use of a breathable finish, such as limewash, is often the most appropriate solution to ensure that damp does not become trapped within the brickwork; this should make an improvement to the performance of the wall, so that the paint removal will have still been worthwhile.

Flint and Pebbles

Flints and pebbles are regional types of building materials that are often associated with coastal areas. Usually they need to be used within panels surrounded by other materials, such as brick or stone, as they are otherwise difficult to build with. Repairs need to be carefully matched to avoid unsightly patches.

The paint finish that has been applied to these decorative brick panels may be causing them to decay underneath. But removing the paint may also damage the brickwork.

This brick plaque may have been painted when repairs were carried out to the surrounding brickwork. Where possible, avoid painting these as moisture may be trapped between the paint surface and the brick, which in the long term may begin to deteriorate.

This is a typical example of pebbles being used within panels of red brickwork.

The stucco or render on this house appears original as the detailing around the window is contemporary with the house.

Rendering one half of a pair of houses changes the overall appearance of the pair.

Stucco and Render

Stucco and render are generally similar and were often self-coloured. However, more recently they may also have been painted, usually with a plastic-based paint that traps any moisture that gets under the surface. The problems arise particularly where this paint finish is not kept well maintained because cracks in the paint can admit water that is not able to evaporate through the paint film. The solutions are either to keep the walls regularly painted or to remove the plastic-based paint (*see* above). Where an

Changing windows and covering the brickwork with render has altered much of the period character of one of this pair of cottages.

The backs of these terraced houses have been rendered at a later date.

Removing render can be difficult and repairs may be necessary to the masonry underneath once the render has been removed.

existing brick or stone house has recently been rendered it may be because repairs have been carried out with non-matching bricks or stones, and so, to unify the appearance or to cover settlement cracks, the walls have been rendered.

Render Repairs

A sample of the existing render may be tested to determine its composition for compatibility, but this may not always be the original one nor the best to use in the circumstances. Where the surrounding render is cracked it may be cleaned out and rerendered. Try to avoid applying render over existing brick or stone walls as this is likely only to create more problems in the future. Further, where the house is one of a group, the architectural balance of the group will be altered. Alterations that affect the house's appearance, such as painting or covering the walls with render, may make a substantial difference, not only to the house itself, its appearance and performance, but also to the appearance of those surrounding it. Where a house is listed or in a conservation area permissions are usually necessary for these types of work, so speak to the conservation officer in the area.

Artificial Stone Features, Paint Removal and Cleaning

Decorative features over windows, doors and bay windows were often made of artificial stone. When these started to weather they were often painted. More recently the paint used is likely to have been a plastic-based masonry paint. The problem is that once any breathable surface is painted with such a paint, water may become trapped between the paint finish and the background. As it is unable to evaporate out again this can lead to decay of the building fabric. It may be possible to remove the paint depending on what was used and how well it has adhered to the background (*see* earlier in this chapter).

The original balustrade above this bay window had been removed and the replacement render has begun to fall off, possibly when the paint finish started to allow water to get in behind it.

These artificial stone lintels above these doors and windows add an interesting contrast to the surrounding brickwork.

The house on the left has had the paint removed from the windows and the door surround.

Where a house forms part of a group the cleaning of one alters the architectural balance of the group.

The lintels over the door and upper windows on the house on the right have been cleaned.

Roughcast and Pebble-dash

Roughcast and pebble-dash are both textured finishes that are applied to walls. With roughcast, small stones are mixed in with the topcoat and thrown at the wall. A later development was pebble-dash, in which small stones are thrown at the topcoat of the render while it is still wet. Pebble-dash was often used as a remedial treatment to disguise repairs. Where a house has been pebble-dashed it may be possible to remove the coating. However, poorly matched brick repairs or enlarged window openings may have been the reason why the house was pebble-dashed in the first place. The removal of pebbledash may not be successful as the bricks may have been gouged out or 'keyed' to provide a rougher surface for the coating to bond to. This may mean that the original brickwork may not be in a sufficiently good condition to be left uncovered if the pebble-dash were to be removed. Try to avoid painting either roughcast or pebble-dash as these create yet another need for maintenance and may also trap damp between an impervious masonry paint finish and the wall beneath. Where a house is listed or in a conservation area permission may again be necessary for these types of work so discuss this with the local conservation officer.

Weatherboarding and Timber-framing

Timber weatherboarding was popular for certain styles of architecture, and breathable stains are often appropriate to keep the timber well maintained and to avoid damp and decay from becoming established. Some of the timber framing used in this period is structural, while in other cases it may only be applied

Roughcast weathers to a natural finish.

to the wall for decorative effect. The most important point is to ensure that any existing paint finish is well maintained, so that water is unable to enter the timber. It can, however, be preferable if the timber is untreated, in which case it may be suitable for oil treatment with 'boiled' linseed oil, or simply stained; if so then it would usually be inappropriate to use any gloss or plastic paint that could risk sealing it up and trapping dampness.

Tile and Slate Hanging

The hanging of tiles or slates on vertical surfaces became popular in Arts and Crafts and Edwardian houses. As these surfaces are often more easily accessible than roofs, they may be the more vulnerable to damage when ladders are leant against them while windows are being cleaned or decorated, for example.

Terracotta

Terracotta is an unglazed, usually brownish-red earthenware used chiefly as an ornamental building material, similar to brick, but with additional

The original brickwork has been pebble-dashed on both these houses and, in addition, the house on the right has also been painted.

Timber weatherboarding is used on the left gable, while timber framing can be seen on the right.

This Westmoreland slate-tile hung gable end is vulnerable to damage if ladders were to be leant against it.

The surrounds to these windows and the balcony are terracotta and are in contrast to the rest of the brickwork.

This door has most of its original features, including the stained glass. A good indication of the age of a door is that a new lock is fitted about every hundred years, old locks on the door are a part of the historical record.

materials mixed in with the clay. Faience is similar to terracotta, but usually has a degree of glazed finish. Terracotta does have a hard, thin 'fireskin' as the outer surface, but, even so, terracotta is a fragile material. If water is able to get into terracotta it is more difficult to repair than brick. In addition, be particularly cautious about trying to clean terracotta as it can easily be damaged, so consult a specialist familiar with this material, and the local conservation officer.

DOORS

There was usually a hierarchy of door types used within the house. The front door was usually the most important one and was often of panelled construction. French windows were sometimes used in rear rooms to allow a greater amount of light to enter, as well as providing access to the garden. Rear doors to sculleries and outbuildings usually had simple, often vertically boarded doors.

To allow light into the front entrance hall, the upper panels of front doors were often glazed, either with stained glass or with plain that may have been frosted or etched. Where space allowed, additional glazing panels were incorporated above and to the sides of the door. Some fanlights above the door were hinged at the bottom so that they opened inwards to allow for ventilation. With the arrival of the postal

LEFT: Paint colours can alter how the house appears.

RIGHT: The type of door used much depended on the surrounding architecture, individually-designed houses were likely to have unique doors, while pattern-books and mass-production would have influenced larger developments.

LEFT: Vertically-boarded doors were often used for passage doors giving access to the rear of a row of houses, rather than panelled doors, as used for entrances.

RIGHT: Doors to the rear of the house were often simple and vertically-boarded, like this to an outbuilding.

system in 1840, letterboxes were incorporated into the front door. Typically, a door would also have a knob and a bell. Sometimes the knocker was incorporated with the letterbox. These pieces of door furniture were usually made of brass, bronze or cast iron that may have been painted. The name or number of the house may have been gilded on to the door itself or on to the fanlight above.

WINDOWS

Sash and bay windows were popular during the earlier part of our period. While later, with the arrival of new architectural styles towards the end of the nineteenth century, casement or side-hinged opening windows, as used in medieval times, began to become

Sash windows give a rhythm to the elevation of this pair of houses.

ABOVE: 'Horns', the moulded piece of timber that project above and below the sash, were necessary to reinforce the sash joints to support the weight of single sheets of glass within a sash frame.

LEFT: The ground-floor sash window is made up of two large sheets of glass that require 'horns', the reinforced angles at the bottom of the top sash. The sash window on the upper floor has intermediate glazing bars that help to strengthen the frame of the window so that it does not require horns on the sashes.

The sashes on the front of this house now have large sheets of glass in them, but the original intermediate glazing bars might perhaps have previously been removed, possibly as a result of changes in fashion, since these sashes do not have horns on them.

Casement windows are hinged at the side and open outwards. These still have the original stained glass in the upper windows.

RIGHT: Some windows had glazing bars that divided the sashes into smaller areas of glass.

BELOW: As fashions changed, glazing bars were often removed to give an unobstructed view through a window. Evidence of this having happened is shown below, where the pieced-in square of timber on the inner sash indicates that the intermediate glazing bar has subsequently been removed.

These ornate casement windows include metal glazing bars for decorative effect.

Decorative details around this splayed bay window add to the individual character of the house.

A decorative upper floor window.

popular again. The vertical sliding sash window was already popular since it was invented at the beginning of the Georgian period. However, early sashes had to have intermediate glazing bars. This was because the crown glass used in early windows could be made only in small pieces. With the development of mechanized glass-manufacturing techniques by the Victorians, much larger sheets of glass could be produced. The ability to have a single sheet of glass within each half of a sash window meant that the corner joints of the sash frame had to be reinforced with projecting 'horns' at the lower or the upper edges to support the weight of the glass. A typical sash window has two vertically sliding sashes attached by sash cords to weights made of either lead or cast iron that hang in concealed timber boxes on either side of the window. The weights balance the weight of the sash so that it stays in a particular position when opened. Sash windows with intermediate glazing bars were often still used at the rear of houses,

Bay windows were often single storey, but they were frequently used on upper stories as well.

Square bay windows were also popular during this period.

These two bay windows add to this elevation.

This is an interesting window detail between two houses.

so that smaller and therefore less expensive sheets of glass could be used where they were less conspicuous.

Generally small dormer windows were normal, but they may have often been enlarged at a later date. In Scotland, larger dormers were often an integral part of the architectural design. Less visible windows, such as roof lights, allow natural light into the middle of a house. They were traditionally placed over the head of the staircase to enable otherwise darker areas to be naturally lit.

ABOVE: Dormer windows are part of the history of a house and were originally designed to be in proportion to the rest of the elevation.

RIGHT: These dormer windows are a typically Scottish detail.

Repairs to Doors and Windows

The timber that was originally used to make the doors and windows was allowed to dry naturally (which is known as seasoning) for much longer than modern timber (which is kiln-dried). This, along with the likelihood that old timber was slow-grown, can mean that the original timber is likely to be more durable than any modern replacement timber, so try to ensure that the original timber is retained. The most vulnerable part of a door or window is the bottom rail since rainwater may splash up from nearby hard surfaces. If the timber is not well protected, by being regularly painted, it may be vulnerable to rot. Where the decay is beyond being halted with decorating fillers, carefully cut out the decayed parts to sound timber and splice in new pieces, but ensure that the splice is cut diagonally to avoid water sitting on the joint line (architraves are similarly susceptible to decay). Doors are prone to swelling in wet weather and may need to be eased by planing a small amount of wood away. Where the bottom of vertical boarding has rotted on a door one

When a sash cord finally rots through, the weight may suddenly drop to the bottom of the sash weight box. This often happens when the window is being opened. It is a fairly easy operation to take the glazed window sashes into the room and renew the cords. To do this, the internal timber bead moulding has to be prized off one of the inner edges of the window. A timber access panel covers the sash weight box, as seen propped up on the side of the cill. These allow access to the compartment which houses the cylindrical metal weights that balance the weight of the sash.

The weights attached to the end of sash ropes to balance the sash or shutter, as in this picture, may become wedged, so wiggling them may free the weight in the sash box.

While this may look bad, it is only the putty that has failed and this can easily be repaired.

Some careful splicing in of new timber to the lower section would allow this window to be repaired before being repainted.

This decay is due to the paint film's cracking and allowing water into the timber. This can often either be repaired with fillers or by splicing in new timber rather than by extensive replacement.

can splice new pieces on to the original boarding rather than replace greater areas of otherwise sound timber.

The most vulnerable windows are usually those in the most exposed locations, such as dormer windows, so examine their interior faces for signs of water damage. Deal with any leaks as soon as they are noticed to avoid more water getting into the fabric of the house, as these types of leak are likely to cause a considerable amount of unseen damage from what may initially have seemed a relatively minor matter.

Although this window has had pieces of timber spliced into it in the past, because the paint film has not been maintained this has allowed rot to become established again and is going to be more extensive and costly to repair.

Replacing putty around the edge of the glass in a window is an easy DIY job and stops water from getting into the timber and causing it to rot and be more expensive to repair in the future.

Decorating Doors and Windows

It is likely that timber windows have been redecorated in the recent past with modern paints that do not breathe. When redecorating over existing paint try to use a breathable or microporous paint that may allow the timber to expand and contract slightly without the paint finish splitting. This type of paint would also allow any moisture to evaporate, so that this reduces the risk of rot beginning. Linseed oil paints that allow the timber underneath to breathe may sometimes be applied over other types of paint and may be as long lasting, although manufacturers may recommend that the existing paint finishes are removed before these paints are applied. The problem with removing paint is that a part of the history of the colour scheme will be lost and there is also a risk of 'rubbing down' moulded detail to the window frame. It is also probable that the underlying layers of paint are lead-based and this means that additional precautions will be necessary (*see* websites). Where a sash window does not open it may be because it was painted shut during a previous redecoration. By cutting the paint finish around the edge of the sash it is sometimes possible to ease the sash open.

*Try to avoid removing old paint using a blow torch as the older layers of paint are likely to be lead-based and require special precautions to deal with them (*see *websites), in addition the historic record of the paint layers would also be destroyed.*

ABOVE: *This original lead paint has cracked into small squares.*

RIGHT: *This is after it had been repainted by using a breathable linseed oil paint.*

ABOVE: Avoid painting the runner where the upper sash slides down to allow it to operate, and apply oil or candle wax to protect the timber instead.

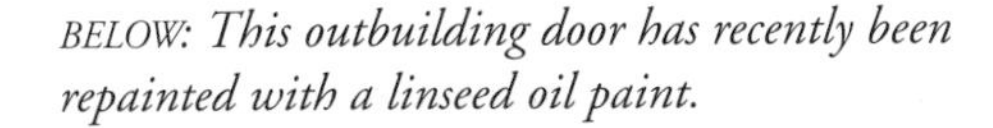

BELOW: This outbuilding door has recently been repainted with a linseed oil paint.

Cast iron rusts if the paint finish is defective; it should be regularly painted to avoid future problems.

Replacement Doors and Windows

Where the existing windows or doors have already been replaced, it is possible to reinstate them with designs that are more in keeping with the originals. However, problems arise where door or window opening have been altered to suit larger windows. This is because it may be quite difficult to find matching bricks or stones to reinstate the original size of the openings. Compliance with current building regulations or standards is usually required, and where a house is listed or in a conservation area

Where replacement windows have been used that are larger than the original size of the window opening, this changes the architectural composition of a group of otherwise similar houses.

These houses, that would originally have looked identical, have been altered in different ways. Both front doors have been replaced with designs that were popular in the last twenty years. Originally the doors would have been four-panelled. The original stone front door threshold step remains on the left house, while that on the right has been replaced. The windows on the left house have been replaced, while those on the right one seem to be the original sash windows (and glass). The slate roof covering appears original on both houses. The black and terracotta, coloured, squared paving tiles are original on both paths. However, that on the left house has been partially replaced by concrete paving slabs. The original stone kerb to the pavement still exists on the left house. The original brick boundary wall in matching bricks to the house still exists on the left. These walls were often made from the rejected bricks from the building of the house. A privet hedge may have been lost on the left, but a hedge is still present in front of the right house, even though this one has a replacement brick wall, as the bricks are different from the house and the wall is slightly lower. It is likely that both houses originally had timber gateposts and gates.

permission is likely to be required so speak to the local conservation officer and building control department for guidance.

GLASS

The Victorians and Edwardians made clever use of glass. They had a range of colours, patterns and designs that made the best use of available light. Victorian glass was machine-made, whereas earlier Georgian glass had been made by hand. There was a noticeable difference in the qualities of these two types of glass at the time, just as there is now between Victorian and modern glass. However, now that modern techniques for producing almost perfectly flat glass exist, the imperfections of Victorian glass seem charming. This means that Victorian and Edwardian glass is not only unique, but it is also difficult to replicate if it is broken. Where a slight rippling effect can be seen in the surface of glass this is likely to be original glass. Stained glass was popular

These replacement windows did not follow the design of the existing windows because they are hinged at the top rather than being vertical sliding sashes, although the size of the window openings has not been altered.

ABOVE: This door has its original stained glass joined together by using thin lead cames I-shaped in section that clasp each side of the glass.

RIGHT: The hall light illuminates this original stained glass.

during this period and used in a variety of styles and designs, but a great deal of this in both doors and windows has been lost over the years. This often happened when the lead that joins the smaller pieces of glass together was damaged and the whole panel was replaced rather than being repaired.

A leaded light is a window formed from small pieces of clear glass, often square or diamond in shape, jointed with lead cames to form larger panels of glass. Patterned and etched glass may be found in doors and windows or in fanlights above doors. The glass fanlight over a front door may also have had gilded letters or numbers on it, and remnants may still be visible.

Where glass has cracked – provided that it is not allowing water in – it might sometimes be appropriate to leave it alone if it is otherwise safe and secure. But where water is getting in there are glass glues that might be used to waterproof the crack, if the glass is otherwise sound. Where the lead between pieces of glass has been damaged it is often possible

Stained glass was used to provide light with privacy to the internal hallway.

This is original etched glass.

Victorian glass is easy to scratch during redecoration.

This is a close-up of some etched glass.

to have small areas of the lead carefully repaired, rather than complete panels re-leaded, as the lead-work itself may be a hand-made work of art in itself. Where any re-leading is being carried out, make sure that all the original glass is reused since any new pieces are likely to be noticeable, because it will probably be difficult to find new pieces that closely match the existing ones.

An important feature of older glass is that it is generally softer than the modern. This means that sanding blocks or scrapers may easily scratch the glass where the adjoining woodwork is being prepared for redecoration; so make sure that the glass is well protected before such works are carried out. Where original glass is missing there may be clues to examples of the original type in nearby houses. Old photographs may also help to identify which windows originally had decorative glass in them. Stained glass and leaded light panels may be vulnerable to a break-in, but to improve them in this respect it may be possible to install a sheet of security glass or metal bars behind them so that the beauty of the glass can still be appreciated instead of replacing them with a uniform sheet of modern glass.

DOOR AND WINDOW FURNITURE

There is a great variety of original door and window furniture that may still be present. Doorknobs were in general use throughout this period and were usually made of brass or iron. Lever door handles

This cast-iron letterbox has been polished with grate polish.

This doorbell pull/push is original, but the doorknob has been replaced with a modern lever handle, to suit a modern mortise lock. It is possible to buy such locks that are deep enough to permit the use of a knob. Doorknobs have to be positioned away from the edge of the door in order to be graspable.

Although time-consuming to paint, timber features like this add to the overall composition of the house.

were often used on Arts and Crafts-inspired houses later in this period. If there is an original bell push, this will usually be in a wall nearby or fixed to a timber doorframe, and probably mechanically operated rather than electrically. On sash windows there are sometimes handles fixed to the underside of upper sashes, to make them easier to open from the outside. Where any original door furniture still remains retain this as part of the history of the house. Where doorknobs have been replaced with modern lever handles, try to choose a new design that is in keeping with the original design of the door. Look at nearby houses of a similar age since this may help with choosing contemporary designs that are appropriate for a particular type of house.

TIMBERWORK

Timber was often used to embellish the front of the house for such features as porches or at high level for bargeboards (decorative timber features covering the 'verges' of gable roofs). To ensure that these features last for many more years without rotting, any modern paint finish has to remain continuous. This means that the timberwork has to be regularly

This timber porch adds to the general appearance of the house and its surroundings.

ABOVE: Porches were sometimes grouped with bay windows.

LEFT: This porch combines timber brackets with a cast-iron decorative detail under the gutter, which should be regularly cleaned out to ensure that water is taken away from the house.

This porch adds to the interest of this house.

The timberwork over this door is a valuable factor in the appearance of this house and should be kept well decorated to ensure that it survives for years to come.

As the blue timber bargeboard on the front part of this gable end is visible from the street, it is more decorative than that to the rear of this house. The paint on the bargeboard might even be long-surviving, lead-based paint; so adequate safety precautions are necessary when its redecoration is being proposed and a paint chosen to provide an equivalent breathable performance.

These decorative bargeboards significantly contribute to the composition of the house and should be carefully redecorated at regular intervals to ensure that they do not begin to rot.

painted to make sure that cracks or splits in the paint surface are not allowed to develop and allow water to enter and cause the underlying timber to rot. When redecoration is being carried out, be aware that the original paint may have been lead-based, so appropriate precautions will be necessary (*see* websites). In theory, breathable paints such as original lead-based or modern linseed oil-based ones will need less frequent renewal since they are less able to trap water in timber. But if any underlying paints are not breathable regular redecoration will be important.

The original timber from this period may well have been of slower growth and seasoning than modern replacement timber that could be more vulnerable if the paint finish deteriorates. As bargeboards are usually difficult to gain access to due to their height above ground, they may not be repainted with the same frequency as other timber elements in the house, even though they may be subject to greater weathering due to their location. It may be worth the cost of stripping out a modern paint and using a good breathable one that will last

Where the original paint is an old lead-based one, it may be appropriate to apply a breathable paint when next redecorations are being planned.

Even if items such as shutters may be a later addition to a house, they are part of its history and should be kept well maintained to avoid their starting to rot.

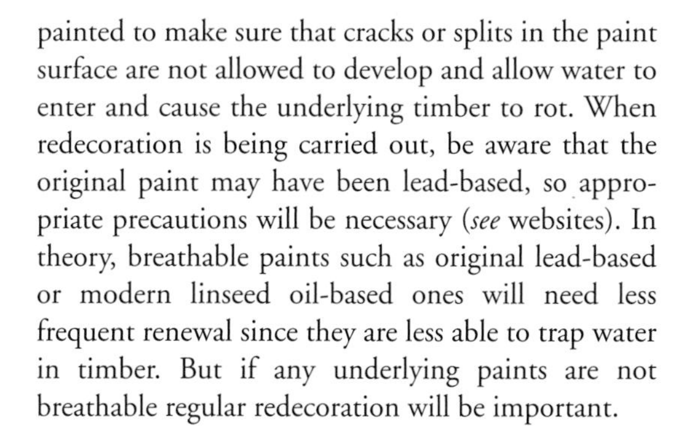

Ensure that timber features like this porch are redecorated regularly, even though this may be time-consuming, to ensure that rot does not become established. Where possible, try to ensure that water is not allowed to splash up from hard surfaces below the timberwork as this may contribute to the base of the timber starting to rot.

This bay window is ingeniously supported by a pair of cast-iron columns that are likely to perform a structural function in this situation.

longer and wear out less harmfully than a conventional modern gloss. Where there are roofs above timber porches make sure that they are regularly checked for signs of leaks and that gutters are regularly cleaned out and checked for leaking joints so that water does not overflow on to the timberwork below and rot it.

A range of cast-iron designs were often used as in this example over a bay window, where a small section is now missing. It would be possible to reproduce this section in cast iron by taking an impression of the existing design and having it reproduced, if it were felt necessary to do so.

IRONWORK

Many houses often have some form of decorative ironwork on them. This can range from balcony rails to features over bay windows. These features are usually made of cast iron, although wrought iron may have been used in some situations (*see* Chapter 5). With all corrodible metalwork, the most important factor is to ensure that it is kept well painted, so that rust is not able to become established. This is particularly important where any of the ironwork performs a structural function. Careful attention should be paid when redecorating to the fixing points with the surrounding structure. This is because other

Where such details as this cast-iron balcony are part of the architectural integrity of both houses, try to paint both sections the same colour.

The original door, wall and floor tiles still survive in this porch. Note also the ventilation holes under the entrance door step that allow air to circulate into the cellar and underfloor voids to keep the timber floors dry and prevent rotting, so make sure that these holes are not blocked.

materials may expand and contract at different rates, so there is a potential for the paint finish to crack or split at this point and let water in. Once water is under the paint finish, rust can become established.

TILES

There were a great number of different designs used on the walls of porches. Where they appear to be missing, look at other houses locally of a similar type to see whether tiles were used in porches, since introducing new tiles is not really appropriate to the setting if the house was built without them.

Perhaps the original tiles will have remained intact over the years, but where they have been damaged the type and the extent of the damage may determine what, if anything, needs to be done. Where the tiles have been painted it may be possible to remove the paint. However, if this is so, this may have been because they were damaged in some way. Trying to find matching replacement tiles is usually difficult. It is often better to leave the damaged tiles as they are

There are a great many designs for tiles in porches, so look around the area to see which ones were popular for specific types of house.

and accept that they are a part of the history of the house. Where it is imperative that repairs should be carried out, they should be repaired *in situ* as by removing them yet more tiles may be damaged. Cracks or missing areas may often be carefully filled and painted over to match the colours of the surrounding tiles.

ENTRANCE STEPS

The materials that were used for entrance steps much depended on the type, style and location of the house. With all these existing elements the aim is to preserve them as they are. They are likely to be damaged when large or heavy objects are moved in or out of the house, so make sure that these areas are carefully protected before any heavy objects are moved over them. It is much more difficult to make a careful and sympathetic repair to steps once they have been damaged.

Avoid the use of waterproof sealants on these surfaces as they are likely to seal in damp and thus contribute to decay. Where impervious coatings have already been applied, they will often have sunk into the treated surface and usually be difficult to remove.

Timber thresholds may survive intact as long as they remain dry, so if they start to show signs of decay, try to find out where the water is coming from that is causing the problem. The causes may range from defective rainwater goods to the lack of an air gap between the house and any adjoining paths, so ensure that where possible there is a gravelled area between the two.

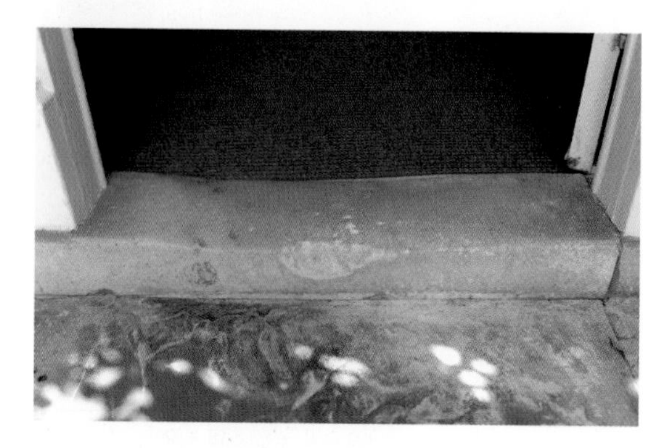

This chipped stone threshold is still a part of the history of the house and would be difficult to repair, but avoid replacing the whole stone threshold as this would destroy a part of this history and waste valuable natural materials in the process.

BOOT SCRAPERS

Boot scrapers were often incorporated into Victorian and Edwardian houses, somewhere near the front door or within a nearby railing.

Original steps may be in many colours and designs, depending on the locality. Where the original covering has already been removed look at similar houses in the area to try and establish what would have been used originally, so as to avoid introducing new elements that are either too decorative or too simple for the original design of the house.

Designs are many and varied.

These steps show the passage of years and enhance the feel of an older house.

These steps show the passage of time.

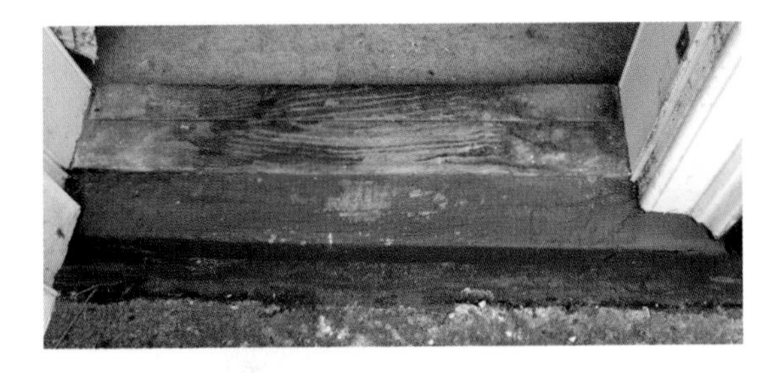

Timber thresholds are more likely to be made from hardwood and are better left undecorated to allow them to breathe.

A boot scraper has been incorporated into the bottom of this railing design.

This is a freestanding boot scraper that would have been set into the ground near the entrance door so that only the red part would have been visible above ground.

ABOVE: A decorative coal-hole cover located in front of the main entrance door to the house and set in a stone slab.

LEFT: This is a fairly plain example of the cover to a coal-hole, others may have been more decorative.

This is the view of a coal chute from inside the cellar, now partially covered by heating pipes.

COAL HOLES

Where a house has a cellar, part of it would have usually been used for coal storage. Circular metal plates may be found somewhere around the perimeter of the house, in accessible locations for coal deliveries. The chutes under these plates enabled the coal to be poured direct into the storage area of the cellar. Where these features still exist, retain them even if coal is no longer used in the house as they are of historical interest.

SERVICES

For a house to function it needs various services brought into it and others to take wastes away. Many houses of this date were built with some or all of the currently available services incorporated into the exterior or the inside of the house. However, with the development of newer services or the greater availability of existing ones, adaptations have often had to be made. This is an on-going process, so where new pipes or cables are to be added their locations and routes should be carefully considered. The aim is to ensure that they have as little visual and physical impact on the existing house as possible. This is achievable provided that the routes of any new services are carefully planned in advance. Where possible, they should be routed well away from the main elevations so that they do not detract from the overall visual impression. Where, for example, a new flue for a boiler or an extractor fan for a kitchen or bathroom is being considered, it should be located in an unobtrusive place, as well as complying with the current regulations (*see* websites). There are other items that may need to be fixed to the house, so give consideration as to where they might go to reduce their impact.

The positioning of security alarm boxes has to be

carefully balanced between their visibility for security reasons and ensuring that the (often brightly coloured) alarm boxes do not spoil the house's appearance. The same applies to television aerials and satellite dishes, which can often be carefully hidden away from the main elevations. Because the visual implications of these items may be significant, permissions may be necessary where a house is listed or in a conservation area, so again contact the conservation officer in your area (*see* websites). Where services are being altered or introduced into a house ensure that the installers are suitably qualified (*see* websites). Where a new gas supply in being installed, a meter enclosure usually has to be positioned somewhere on the house exterior. Select an unobtrusive type and locate it well away from the main elevation. Where a house is listed or is in a conservation area official consents may be required from the local authority.

Try to avoid increasing the amount of external illumination and thus reduce local light pollution. The light in the entrance hall often illuminated the exterior path though a glass fanlight. As most existing light fittings are now usually adaptable for use with low-energy lamps, use these to save energy – but check for compatibility where these may be used with sensors. Where movement detectors activate lights, site them discreetly and ensure that the sensors are positioned to activate the light when someone is walking up the path to the house rather than along the street. Where older light fittings still remain, even if they are disused, these are a part of the history of the house. But when choosing new ones, make sure that they look appropriate to the house. For inspiration, start by looking at nearby, similar houses to see what types of light fitting have been used there to see which ones most enhance the setting of the house.

These satellite dishes have an impact on the elevations.

The entry door still has its original stained glass, but the gas meter would ideally be better sited elsewhere.

ABOVE: This collection of gas-meter enclosures changes the emphasis of this group of houses, which otherwise retains many original features.

RIGHT: This is a more discreet type of gas-meter enclosure.

CHAPTER 4

Interior

The interiors of many houses have been altered over the years and it is rare that all of the original features survive. However, when some do they should be carefully looked after to maintain the original character and qualities of the house. This will ensure that they are preserved for future generations to appreciate. Where features have already been removed, this paradoxically is also a part of the history of the house and demonstrates how the house has developed over time. However, if the decision is made to reinstate features such as missing cornices, for example, then consider an appropriate contemporary design that contributes towards the continuing history of the house. This will also alert any future historians to the fact that alterations have taken place rather than conceal them by using copies of designs that may or may not have been part of the house originally. Where a house is listed, the listing will include all interior features, and so, whether choosing to reinstate a period scheme or opting for a sympathetic modern interpretation, start by speaking to your local conservation officer.

This is a Gothic-inspired balustrade with original Victorian textured wallpaper below the mid-height dado rail on the wall behind.

HISTORICAL COLOUR SCHEMES

As most interiors will have been redecorated on a number of occasions, there will usually be little that remains of former colour schemes. But by looking for clues about past colours this may help to influence the direction that a new colour scheme may take. When starting to consider what might be suitable for the house, try to find out as much as possible about the colours and wallpapers that were used earlier. The places to look for such clues are areas that have not been decorated for a while – these might include the backs of cupboards or under light switches. Leftover rolls of wallpaper may have been used to line cupboards and drawers, so do not assume that a particular wallpaper was used where it has been found.

In the principal rooms and hallways there may have been several complimentary designs of paper used on the same wall, so check at different heights to see whether the same paper was used all over or just on certain areas. Pay particular attention to the areas

Where the top coat of paint has lifted this has revealed a grained and varnished finish that was often applied to soft woods to give the appearance of a hardwood such as oak.

The inside of this cupboard door reveals that the outside, now painted white, would also have been grained like this in the past.

above and below where a picture rail may have been, as different designs may have been used in the two places. A similar distinction may be apparent above and below where a dado rail may have been, which would be around waist height. Many rooms were often papered over with newer papers as fashions changed, so there may be a build up of several layers on one wall. If old wallpapers are found they may be dated by comparing them with examples found in books of wallpaper patterns from the period. Otherwise take a photograph of the paper and send it to a specialist wallpaper manufacturer – they may be able to suggest a close alternative if they do not have an exact match. Where any remaining pieces of a wallpaper are sufficiently large it may be reproducible, but this is usually a fairly expensive option.

The more elaborate and expensive designs may have been used in the principal rooms and cheaper ones used in the bedrooms, for example. Kitchens and bathrooms were usually painted until washable wallpapers became available. The earliest wallpapers had a fairly small pattern repeat, because the printing rollers were smaller on the printing machines of the period. Larger pattern repeats were possible only once larger printing rollers were developed later. Another pointer to the date of wallpapers is that the edges were cut by hand before being pasted into position, whereas modern papers from about the 1960s onwards have ready-cut edges. Wallpapers were traditionally hung using a flour-based paste that included other ingredients to inhibit mould growth, but be aware that some modern wallpaper pastes may also inhibit the breathability of the walls. When emulsion paints became popular in the middle of the twentieth century it was often easier to paint over existing wallpapers rather than to remove them. This means that if a paper becomes unstuck, there may be historical clues beneath it. Sometimes a powdery paint finish may be found under later layers and this may possibly be distemper (an earlier type of paint more breathable than modern emulsion paints and this is still available; *see* Chapter 2).

Other clues as to earlier paint colours that were used may be found where internal joinery such as doors, windows and cupboards has been chipped, revealing what is below. While brown-coloured wood graining went in and out of fashion on doors, windows and other timberwork during this period, most houses now have had modern paint finishes applied over them. However, where there are areas of the original paint finish these are a valuable historical record and should be preserved.

As well as looking carefully at the house, try to broaden the research by looking at similar houses

This sample of wallpaper was found in the back of a cupboard where the walls around it had already been painted with a modern emulsion paint.

Another area of rectangularly-shaped wallpaper was found in the same cupboard under the diamond-shaped paper. Neither may necessarily have been used in this room, but elsewhere in the house.

nearby as they may yield clues about the colour schemes used in particular types of house at certain dates. Where existing paints or wallpapers are still present, particularly if they are old examples, these are often unique features to appreciate. Where woodwork has revealed earlier colour schemes as a result of chipped paint these may be appropriate to use as the basis for new colour schemes. As the colours that were sometimes used in the past were generally much darker than those favoured now, where the earlier colours are not now considered to be appropriate, try to make sure that there are sufficient indicators of previous colour schemes present so that if a future occupant wishes to recreate the earlier schemes they will be able to do so. Whether or not matching earlier colour schemes, an important consideration can be to select paints and wallpapers that are breathable (*see* Chapter 2).

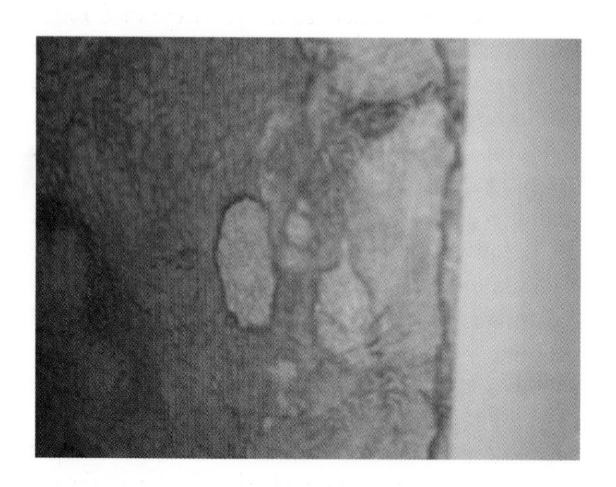

This wallpaper was also found in a cupboard, and, even though it is not contemporary with the building of the house, it is still part of its history.

Embossed papers were popular during this period and this is an example of a frieze paper above a picture rail in an entrance hall.

ABOVE: Embossed papers were also popular for use below dado rails, as seen here below the rail on this staircase.

RIGHT: A small patch of embossed paper still remains on this upper floor landing, so ensure that such historical details are retained for future reference.

CEILINGS

Victorian and Edwardian ceilings were usually constructed of lath and plaster, in which timber laths (strips of timber) were fixed to the timber ceiling joists above and plaster applied to them (see Chapter 2). A lath and plaster ceiling may undulate very slightly since it was handcrafted into position. By looking down on the ceiling from the floor void or attic above it is usually possible to determine the type of ceiling construction. There may also be sound-deadening material in the floor void to reduce noise transmission between rooms on different floors. Looking under this material may give clues about the ceiling construction below. With an original lath and plaster ceiling the laths are usually visible, with lumps of creamy-coloured plaster visible where it has been squeezed through between the laths from below to form a secure fixing or key for the plaster. While expanded metal mesh was beginning to be used during this period as a substitute for timber, it has been more widely used during the twentieth century as a remedial measure. If the back of the ceiling appears to be a flat board covered with paper or foil, this is likely to be a replacement plasterboarded ceiling.

Plasterboard was developed after expanded metal lathing and is a factory-made product, in which plaster is sandwiched between two sheets of paper, one of which may be foil-backed. A foil backing was used to reflect heat as well as being a vapour barrier, which may conflict with the aim of allowing old houses to breathe. Sometimes the original lath and plaster ceiling may have been left in place and a new plasterboard ceiling applied over the surface where it has begun to crack or sag. This was not always a good idea because this can impose an extra weight on the plasterboard ceiling below. A new plasterboarded ceiling usually has a uniform and flat appearance. The joints between boards are filled and painted or they may have been covered with tape and then a thin layer or 'skim coat' of modern gypsum (often of a pink colour) plaster applied by hand over the whole ceiling. Plasterboard is often used to replace lath and

This straight-line crack indicates that this ceiling has been replaced with plasterboard because cracks in lath and plaster ceilings tend to be more random.

plaster ceilings, either as a cheaper material or because the builders lack the necessary skills. Where it has been used it contrasts sharply with the handmade qualities of an original lath and plaster ceiling.

Ceiling Roses

The original purpose of ceiling roses was to disguise the smoke blackening from candles, oil or gas lamps, they could easily be repainted without touching the rest of the ceiling. They were also used as a decorative feature in the principal reception rooms to enhance the setting of the central light fitting. Some ceiling roses may have been perforated to assist ventilation in conjunction with vents in the external walls where gas lamps were in use.

Cornices

Cornices, which have a practical function to cover the junction between the wall and ceiling, are usually found in entrance halls, reception rooms and the principal bedrooms, but are less common in functional rooms, such as kitchens and bathrooms, or in basements and attic rooms that may have been used by servants. Within a house there is usually a hierarchy of designs, so that, for example, a reception room would have a more ornate cornice than a bedroom. There were two methods of making a plaster cornice: either they were 'run' *in situ* at the house or run or moulded in lengths on a workshop bench and then cut to size when being fitted in a

This ceiling rose still retains much of its original detail despite having been painted many times, but, as distemper has been used, this can easily be brushed off the mouldings so that the details do not become clogged with paint.

This ceiling rose has been painted over many times, but the decorative details are still visible.

A new plaster cornice being run by hand.

room. In both cases the cornice was made by building up layers of lime and, particularly for workshop-made versions, plaster of Paris, with a shaped template in reverse, to achieve the final profile of the moulding. Any decorative embellishments, such as flowers or motifs, were then fixed to the cornice.

Where a cornice has been damaged repairs are possible by using the same materials as the original ones, so carefully examine the broken areas to see what they are made from. If long sections of cornice are missing, new pieces may be made to match by using the original profile as a template. Where there is evidence to suggest that a cornice previously existed but has since been lost there are many new and traditional patterns still available. When choosing a new cornice, be aware of the scale and the relative

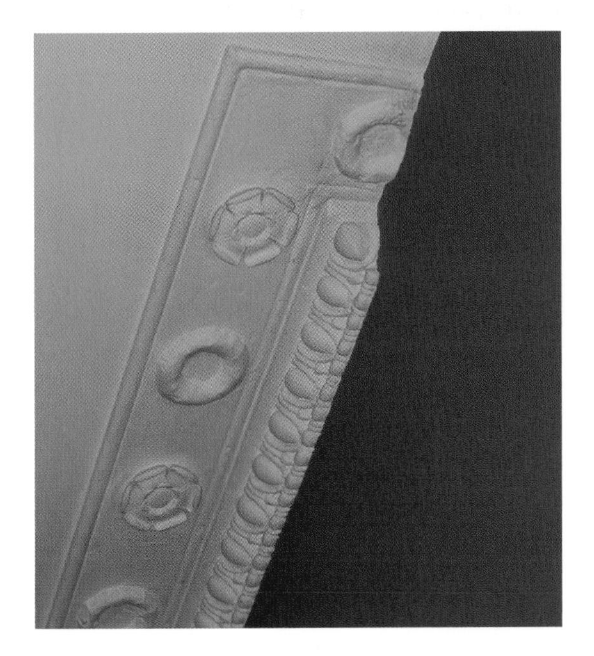

Decorative features were often fixed to a cornice after it had been made.

This reception room cornice has additional detailing applied to the ceiling to enhance its appearance.

The rose, cornice and picture rail frieze enliven this room.

Plaster brackets typically framed the dropped beam in many entrance halls.

importance of the room to avoid being too fussy or having too plain a design. The best way of establishing what would be the most appropriate is to look at similar houses to gain an idea of the proportions and styles used within similar sized rooms.

Plaster Features

Where there is a possibility that other plaster features may be missing do some research to establish whether the house originally had them and, if so, how simple or elaborate they may have been. This is to ensure that any new details are in keeping with the house rather than being over- or under-stated.

Ceiling Papers

Ceilings may have been covered with decorative papers ranging from embossed papers of the nineteenth century to the woodchip papers popular in the

There were a great many designs used for cornices during this period, but the same type of decorative detailing might be found in similar houses of around the same date in the same area.

This original entrance hall design is intact.

Woodchip paper was often used in the latter half of the twentieth century to cover cracks. The white-painted wall above the picture rail and the ceiling have woodchip paper on them, while the yellow-painted wall below the picture rail is an older, lightly embossed wallpaper that has been painted.

mid-twentieth century. Original decorative papers are a part of the history of the house, so look after them where they are found. Some traditional patterns may still be available that match or complement the original ones. Later additions to ceilings, such as woodchip paper, are also part of house's history, but are also usually an indicator that there were cracks in the ceilings as these were usually fairly easily concealed with such paper. Removing any of these later textured papers may reveal additional problems.

Textured Ceiling Finishes

The use of textured ceiling finishes was popular from the 1960s onwards. They were usually applied with brushes, combs or rollers, depending on the final pattern and design that was required. However, the purpose of such finishes in older houses was often to conceal cracks in existing ceilings. Some of these textured finishes contained asbestos, so it is a sensible precaution to have these materials tested before carrying out any works. Often it may be easier to leave the finishes in place and plaster over them to obtain a smoother finish, rather than to disturb them as they can be difficult to remove. If they do contain asbestos seek official advice on how to identify them for future reference and on what precautions to take in the meantime when working around them; such activities as drilling and cutting the surfaces should be avoided (*see* websites).

Downlighter Light Fittings

Where downlighters have been recessed into lath and plaster ceilings the laths have usually been cut to accommodate them, but unfortunately this reduces the structural integrity of the ceiling because the cut ends of the laths are then unsupported. The light bulbs in these fittings create quite high temperatures, so there is a potential fire risk within floor voids that may also be full of debris. In addition, fire, smoke, draughts and sound may also be able to travel between rooms on different floors as the continuous ceiling finish has been perforated. Where these fittings have already been installed, the fitting of energy-efficient, low-energy or LED lamps may reduce the amount of heat generated within the

Avoid inserting downlighters into lath and plaster ceilings as they damage the structural integrity of the ceiling and can be a fire hazard; they could also create and transmit fire and smoke as well as reducing sound insulation between floors.

ceiling void. As an additional fire (and acoustic) precaution, special covers are available to place around these fittings within the ceiling void, though these should not themselves be allowed to cause overheating and manufacturers may likely need to be consulted.

Repairing Ceilings and Plaster Features

Bulges and cracks in lath and plaster ceilings usually indicate that there may be a problem with the adhesion of the plaster to the laths. The most common cause of this is that the slender hooks of plaster that hold it firmly against the laths are broken, and this may result in the ceiling starting to sag. A heavy object being dropped on the floor above may cause these plaster hooks to break and, in the long term, the weight of the unsupported ceiling to create a bulge.

Another problem connected with ceilings arises where water comes into contact with the laths. This may be as a result of water leaking from radiators or pipework in the area above the ceiling, or from roof, gutter or downpipe leaks or blockages. Where there is no ventilation to allow the laths to dry out, the laths or the plaster may start to decay. In time this may lead to the plaster beginning to sag and, as a consequence, pieces of the ceiling may eventually start to fall off.

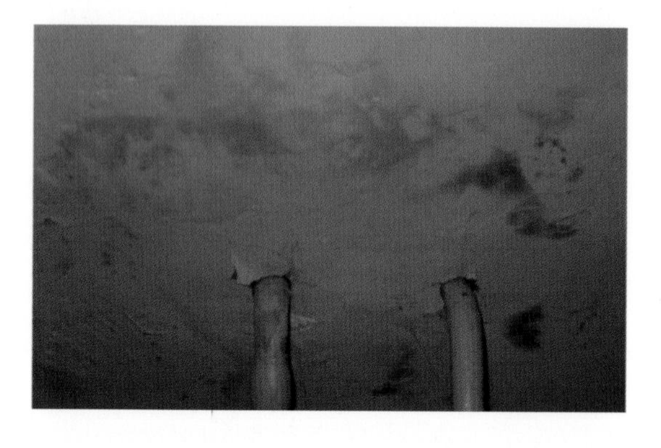

These damp stain marks are from a bath overflowing in the room above, rather than a persistent leak, so establish what has happened before deciding on how to deal with the situation.

Before considering how to approach the repairs, the cause of the leak needs to be dealt with. The area must then be allowed to dry out naturally for as long as possible and this usually means introducing as much ventilation as possible. The necessary repairs may be many and varied and depend upon the initial problem. The types of solution adopted may range from using wire threaded through the ceiling from above to support it where the hooks of the plaster ceiling have been broken off, to replastering with a similar mix to the existing one, where areas of the ceiling are missing. Where areas are to be replastered, the underlying laths have to be securely fixed in place and so repairs may be necessary to these before any replastering may be carried out. When approaching a ceiling repair, as with any other, retain as much as possible of the existing fabric and use materials compatible with the original construction to avoid any new cracks occurring where different types of material expand and contract at different rates. Designing and carrying out these repairs is usually a specialist task, so ask the conservation officer at the local authority as they may be able to make suggestions.

Where individual pieces of plaster have broken off or are missing from decorative plaster details, such as ceiling roses or plaster brackets, it may be more appropriate to leave them as they are part of the history of the house. However, where the missing pieces are noticeable then it is possible to have new pieces modelled and fixed in place, but this should be considered only if the missing details detract from the overall design.

New Plaster Features

Where original features, such as decorative cornices, are missing and there is conclusive evidence that they have been removed, if it is felt appropriate, they may be reinstated. But consider a new design as an alternative to a replica of an existing feature. This is so that future historians are able to identify that a cornice is new rather than being original.

Decorating Ceilings and Cornices

Many ceilings and cornices will have been repainted over the years and some of the details of the embellishments or of the overall design may have been obscured. Traditionally, ceilings and cornices were

The original cornice in this reception room has been lost and this is a new, fibrous, plaster cornice.

This original cornice remained in an adjoining room to that shown on the left.

This new, fibrous, plaster ceiling rose has been added to a room where the original was missing.

The back of this new ceiling rose indicates that it was made traditionally by using fibrous plaster on a reinforcing web of hessian across a timber frame.

Try to establish what the ceiling and walls were painted with before considering what type of paint to use for redecoration.

painted with distemper, a chalk-based paint. The type often used on ceilings is known as 'soft' distemper since it does not need any other ingredients in it such as oil, which would make it slightly less powdery, but also slightly less breathable. A powdery finish is only less satisfactory where there is the possibility that clothes may come into contact with it. When a ceiling was painted with distemper it was possible to wash it off before the next redecoration. This meant that the details of the plasterwork may have remained crisp and well defined. Distemper was, however, often simply reapplied. This means that with the build up of layers of it, which were then often later covered with layers of emulsion paint, many of the original details may have become obscured. Sometimes a thin layer of emulsion creates a skin that can be peeled away from the underlying soft, powdery distemper. However, where distemper and emulsion have fused together then this is much more difficult to remove. Where emulsion paint has been used, a distemper might sometimes successfully be applied over it to give a much more individual character to the paint finish. To remove emulsion from finely detailed mouldings may be difficult and time consuming, but try to avoid any repainting by using emulsion paint as this is likely to increase the build up of paint on the mouldings and make future removal even more difficult.

If you are considering the removal of emulsion paint from an unpapered ceiling or a cornice, there is no guarantee that all of it may be removed. Where areas of paint are already flaking away this indicates that there is poor adhesion to the lower layers of paint. In rooms that have been subject to higher moisture content, such as kitchens and bathrooms, emulsion paint may be more difficult to remove from distemper. However, it may be possible to remove the paint by angling a paint scraper under the surface of the flaking emulsion and separating it from the distemper. If this does not work, moistening the surface may help to loosen the emulsion paint. The final option to try is a steamer, but as this is likely to soften decorative details as well as the paint, great care is needed.

While some forms of decoration may be more robust, other materials may have been used that are softer than the underlying plaster. These include papier mâché which was used for some decorative details applied to the plaster surface. In these situations the plaster or the decorative details may be more easily damaged with a paint scraper or destroyed if treated with too much water. When trying to remove paint from such details there may come a point where it may be less damaging to leave the remaining paint on and to repaint with distemper. A further stage might be to try some form of environmentally-friendly chemical paint-removal method, but this may damage the details further if not carefully managed and neutralized.

WALLS

The majority of external and internal walls are usually of brick or stone that is then plastered to create a smooth internal finish. Some non-load-bearing internal walls, especially on the upper floors, may have been constructed of timber. These partitions are made of vertical timber 'studs' and horizontal timber 'noggins' that keep the structure rigid. Horizontal timber laths are nailed to either side of the studs and plastered on both sides, in a similar way to lath and plaster ceilings. If floorboards run under an internal wall, this might indicate that it is timber-framed. A timber partition wall usually sounds hollow by comparison with a solid wall. A variety of infill materials may have been used within the timber framing to improve the sound insulation between adjoining rooms. Internal timber-framed walls may also form part of the load-bearing wall system within the house, so before considering any alterations, ensure that the structure is fully understood. The inner face of some external masonry walls may also sound hollow when tapped because the walls may have been 'dry-lined' in which an air gap has been created between the outer and the inner wall by using timber battens to which a plaster finish has been applied. This may be either part of the original construction or later remedial work. Where this is likely to be a later alteration it may mean that there has been a damp problem with the walls in the past. An indication of this may be the air vents often found in this type of wall as they enable air to circulate and allow damp to evaporate. Blocking up the vents in these situations may lead to serious decay.

Repairs to Walls

To retain the character of the house try to preserve all the internal plasterwork since this is part of the history of the house. Where there are already holes in plastered walls they are easily repaired by using a similar mix to the original. Typically, plaster was made from lime and sand in roughly a one to three ratio and was usually applied in two or three coats, with animal hair mixed into the lower coats for reinforcement. Where the repairs are to a timber-stud partition wall, ensure that the existing laths are firmly secured in place before applying new plaster. Where the existing laths are broken, these should be secured back in place to provide a firm basis for the new plaster. Where walls have recently been repaired, gypsum plaster, which is often pink in colour, or grey cement renders might have been used. These types of plaster will have different characteristics from an original lime plaster. Gypsum might hold in dampness and salts, while cement renders may introduce an impervious barrier that reduces the migration of damp out of the fabric. Where these modern plasters have previously been used to repair a wall, they tend to crack at the junction with the original plaster. This is because they expand and contract at different rates from the original plaster and behave differently in the presence of moisture. For this reason it is more sensible to use materials that are similar to the original ones, and therefore more compatible for repairs, so that problems such as differential movement and imperviousness are avoided.

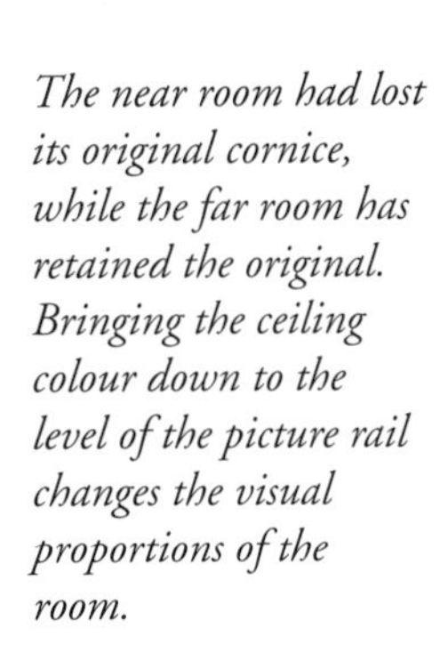

The near room had lost its original cornice, while the far room has retained the original. Bringing the ceiling colour down to the level of the picture rail changes the visual proportions of the room.

Decorating Walls

When approaching the redecoration of walls try to establish what types of paint or wallpaper have already been used. Where modern emulsion paints have been applied, these are usually not very breathable because of the plastic-based materials in them. Where the walls have not been redecorated for many years, they may have originally been painted with an older, relatively breathable paint or distemper. In these situations it is sensible to use distemper or the most breathable of emulsion paints currently available. Trade decorators use a slightly more breathable type of emulsion paint on newly plastered, modern, internal walls, which may be appropriate. Another option is to choose more environmentally-friendly paints, but check their specification to make sure that they are breathable as well as being environmentally-friendly as these two qualities do not necessarily go together. The most breathable and traditional type of wall paint originally used in this period was distemper. This is a chalk-based paint that can be very breathable, provided it not does include oils or some other additives. The reason that oils were often added is that distemper may powder when touched, so the oil makes it more resistant to wear.

This may also be a part of the reason why such features as a dado – the area between a mid-height dado rail and the skirting board below – might be tiled, timber-panelled or simply painted with a less powdery paint finish that did not brush off on clothes. If any distemper remains on the walls, then consider using this again since there will be subtle variations in its texture and in how it reflects light that emulsion paint lacks due to the uniformity of the product. Ordinary 'soft' distemper is also very good at filling minor cracks. Spillages can usually be cleaned up easily, so it is quite DIY-friendly. Other similarly breathable paints that may be found are whiting, made from chalk, or limewash that is made by diluting lime putty with water. These types of paint also have a powdery finish like distemper that enhances the quality of light reflected in this type of finish. All these types of paint were tinted with powdered pigments to achieve the desired colour.

Where walls have been papered with wallpapers with a vinyl finish, they do not allow the wall behind to breathe properly. So, where possible, replace these with papers that have a more breathable finish. In addition, be careful to consider the type of paste that was used to fix the wallpaper to the walls as this too may have waterproof qualities. Also be careful about having a wall 'sized' before it is papered, as this usually means that two rather stronger coats of paste are applied to the wall and allowed to dry before the paper is hung. These coats of paste tend to inhibit the migration of damp out of the walls, so any present becomes trapped, unable to evaporate naturally and may cause further problems. Where a room is likely to be subject to high levels of moisture, such as kitchens or bathrooms, wallpaper may not be the most appropriate finish, as the edges may start to lift off.

Wall Tiles

Perhaps the most common place for tiles to be found on walls was in the kitchen or scullery area where they were functional and invariably white. Decoration may have been introduced around the edges with smaller tiles in contrasting colours. Where any original tiles do remain be careful to retain them as part of the history of the house. Try to avoid regrouting the joints as they are usually very narrow and the edges of the tiles may be chipped off by accident during this process.

White tiles were often used in kitchens and bathrooms.

INTERNAL DOORS

The most typical design of internal door during this period was the four-panel model, but five- and six-panel doors may be found in certain places or in particular types of house. Pairs of panelled doors were sometimes used between reception rooms to give greater flexibility. Half-glazed doors could be used as inner entry doors in halls or to kitchens and for lobbies. Vertically-boarded, solid timber doors, often known as ledged and braced doors, were used for more functional rooms, such as pantries and cellars.

Solid Doors

The hierarchy of internal doors is usually identified by the elaborateness of the mouldings around the door panels. The most important doors within the house, as for reception rooms, may have more elaborate mouldings than for doors on the upper floors. Former service areas often did not have any mouldings on the door at all. Instead, they just had the square edges of the door panel visible. Over the years doors may have been rehung on the opposite side of the door frame, as fashions changed over which way they opened. The original intention seemed to have been to screen the room on opening the door, and this may have also helped to keep draughts from disturbing the fire. Where a door has been rehung there may be impressions of let-in pieces of timber having been used to cover the old hinge positions or where locks have been repositioned.

Glazed Doors

There were two main types of half-glazed door used during this period. A typical pattern had nine panels of glazing in the upper half. These types of door were used for inner doors in entry halls, lobbies or to kitchens. However, a simpler form of glazing was used for other doors, where the upper two solid panels of a four-panel door were replaced with glass. In both cases this allowed 'borrowed light' into otherwise less well lit areas. The type of glass used

RIGHT: This is a typical four-panel door with mouldings around each panel.

FAR RIGHT: This door is to a service room and so does not have a decorative moulding around the edge of the panels. The door still has its original rectangular patch lock and handle.

ABOVE LEFT: Doors to smaller rooms or cupboards may not have had mouldings on the room side of the door, even where there were mouldings on the hall side.

ABOVE: These ledged and braced doors in cellars still have their original, possibly lead-based, paint finish.

LEFT: This ledged door was made without using diagonal cross braces; it still retains its original hinges and patch lock as well as an early paint finish.

This lobby door has nine unequal panels of glass.

These nine equal panels of glass allow light into this front entrance lobby when the main front door is open.

in these doors was generally obscured, patterned or coloured. Where the glass was either etched or patterned one side of it was usually smooth. Where a door retains its original glass be careful to ensure that it is looked after since it may be difficult to obtain matching glass. In addition, retaining the original glass is also about retaining a part of the house's history. Where the glass has been cracked, there are several repairs that may be appropriate. There are glass glues that may be suitable for use, depending on the situation and circumstances. Alternatively, a safety film may be applied over the glass. However, if the film becomes fused to the glass over time this may become a non-reversible process and so this may be appropriate only as a last resort. Even so, this is preferable to replacing the glass, as this would mean that the original was lost forever.

These doors have etched glass upper panels and 'borrowed lights' above to allow light into an otherwise dark lobby.

A four-panel door with a glass fanlight above allows 'borrowed light' into the passage, while maintaining privacy within the room.

This is a typical design for doors for kitchen and service areas that allows light into otherwise gloomy areas.

Door and Window Furniture

The fittings on doors and windows are collectively known as 'door furniture' and 'ironmongery'. Doorknobs rather than levers were used on internal doors and they were usually made of brass. A popular design incorporated a ribbed pattern around them that, as well as being decorative, made them easier to grip. Other materials such as iron, wood and china may also be found as original door furniture. Door lever handles may be found in Arts and Crafts-styled houses and are often made of brass, copper or iron. They are more fragile than doorknobs and the lever mechanisms tend to wear over time. A later development was the use of Bakelite, a plastic with a slightly mottled brown finish. This was often used as a replacement for earlier door furniture, when it became fashionable, and is now of mainly historical interest. Two particular types of door lock were common during this period: rectangular patch locks, fitted to one side of the door and usually made of brass, iron or covered with a timber casing. The other type that was then popular was the mortice lock set within the thickness of the door.

There are many other pieces of furniture that may have been fixed to doors over the years, often as a result of changing trends in fashions and which may have since been removed. One example is fingerplates that were usually placed above but sometimes below

ABOVE: Glass of several colours and patterns was used in various locations.

RIGHT: This door has a combination of dates of glass in it. The reeded, clear glass edge panels and the red-coloured glass corner panels are original Victorian, but the centre panel is a late twentieth-century replacement of patterned safety glass as it has a British Standards kite mark stamped on it. The square corner panels in this design of door were often of coloured glass or alternatively of decorative etched glass.

Detail of original reeded glass in the door illustrated above.

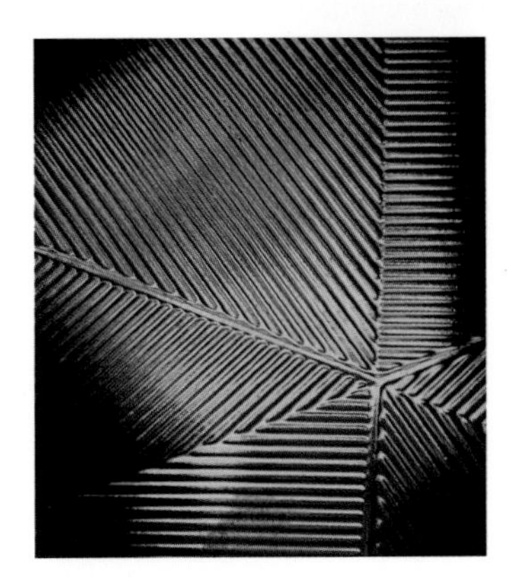

Detail of replacement pressed patterned safety glass.

Detail of original red-coloured glass corner panels.

the handle to protect the door, as well as being a form of decoration. It may still be possible to see the impression of their former positions in certain lights. Other features that may still exist or have been removed are escutcheon plates; these cover the keyholes for locks set within the thickness of the door. Such covers also reduce an admittedly small, but nevertheless important source of draughts. Many doors may still have their original door bolts, so make use of these in addition to any later ones that have been added.

Some fanlight windows above doors may open

This is a popular design of rectangular patch lock, but there were many shapes and sizes, so retain any that still exist as a part of the house's history.

This is an Edwardian lock on a rear door, with an original ribbed door handle.

inwards, as they are hinged at the bottom and may still have the original metal stays in place that limit the amount that the window was able to open. Even if the window is no longer used, the retaining of these stays helps to identify the original function of the window. Windows usually have fewer pieces of furniture on them. But the minimum that a sash window usually has is a security device that locks the two sashes by slightly squeezing them together; this is called a 'sash fastener'. There were three popular designs available during this period: the lever which pivoted sideways into the closed position; a screw fitting that lifted up to open it; or a circular plate that turned sideways to squeeze the lock shut. Pairs of brass hooks or recessed handles may still be present on the lower sash to help to pull it up. Where original or earlier door and window furniture still remains it forms part of the history of the house and should be

Latches as well as doors may have been swapped around in the house over time and may appear to be upside down or have acquired new door knobs.

Most internal doors had locks on them which were either fitted on to the face of one side of them or fitted or morticed within the thickness of the door, as here; so a cover or 'escutcheon' plate is not only decorative but may reduce the draughts through the keyhole.

This original ribbed door handle and cover plate to the key hole still remain on this door.

retained. Much original furniture will have often been often been lost since it is easily removed when redecorating is being carried out and is either renewed or not refixed. The catches on sash windows may have broken over the years. Where a new sash fastener is necessary try to retain the original one on the window for posterity. With side-opening casement windows the opening handle is vulnerable as great pressure is often exerted on it when trying to close the window, especially if it is slightly swollen with the wet. A popular design of window fastener is known as a 'monkey tail' because of its curled handle. In order to prevent casement windows from swinging in the wind, they usually have stays to hold them open, these also help to give additional leverage when tying to close the window.

Most pieces of door and window furniture are repairable, provided that some careful research is carried out to establish what needs to be done and who is the most appropriate person to do it. Where keys are missing from locks a knowledgeable person can make new ones for an existing lock. Alternatively, an old key may be found that works the lock, by trial and error, as there were often standard types available. When trying to make locks work again, try using graphite (pencil lead) because oil clogs up the action and attracts dust. Hinges may begin to wear in time, but these may be adjusted, depending on what is causing the problem. Even where new hinges are necessary, try wherever possible to retain the originals on the door as part of the history. Full-height window doors that are known as French windows often have espagnolette locking bolts, which are clever devices to secure the door simultaneously at the top and the bottom by turning a central knob. These are rare pieces of door furniture to survive. Where new security locks are to be fitted to doors and windows, consider where they are to be located so that the existing furniture is retained as well. When fitting new security locks to windows try to avoid disturbing the timber joints as this will weaken the frame. When fitting new locks try to remove as little as possible of the original timber for structural reasons and also consider the visual impact of new security locks both to doors and windows and choose those that do not detract from the overall appearance.

Old bolts like this are part of the history of the house.

This is an elaborate example of a 'monkey tail' window fastener.

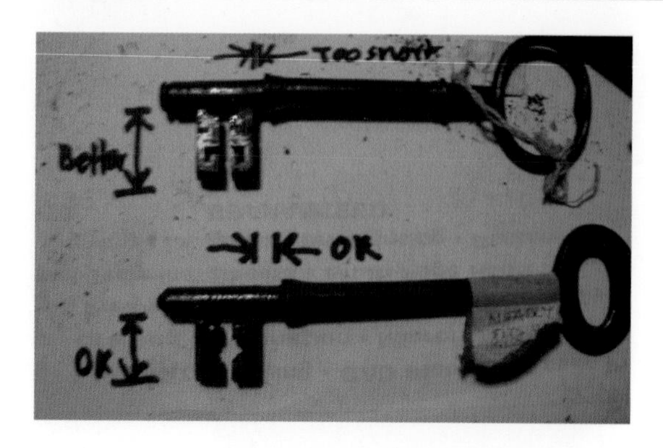

Trial and error is one way to find an old key that works on an old lock to bring it back into use.

Although the plastic Bakelite was a later invention, any door handles or door furniture that remain have historical value.

Repairs to Doors and Windows

Internal doors do not usually require a great deal of repair. The most common problems are caused by damp in the surrounding areas that may affect the door, or when a door has been slammed and the joints become loose. The bottoms of doors were often cut off to accommodate thicker floor finishes, such as fitted carpets. Where there is a gap under a door, a matching sized piece of timber may be fixed to the bottom of the door to reduce draughts, if more temporary measures such as upholstered draught strips are not being used. When a door starts to get damp it begins to expand slightly and may then become difficult to open or close. This may be just a short-term, seasonal problem, but, if it persists, then the door can be planed to make it close more easily. However, it is always sensible to paint any exposed timber since further damp is more likely to be attracted to unpainted timber, if the rest of the door has an impervious paint finish on it. Possibly one of the most unfortunate things that can happen to a door occurs if paint is removed by the door's being dipped in a chemical bath, since this could loosen the joints within the door and cause gaps to open up at these points. If there are damaged areas of timber they can easily be repaired by carefully piecing in the minimum of new timber. If mouldings around the panels are missing the profile of the existing ones can be matched in new timber and then pinned back into position. As a great many varieties of moulding were used, finding an exact match from a standard range is usually difficult. Where central heating is being installed in a house for the first time, try to introduce the heat slowly so that the doors become gently accustomed to the change as the timber dries out, as this can help to prevent the door panels from cracking.

The most vulnerable part of a window is usually the bottom edge, where rainwater may splash up from the window cill below, or where water cannot drain away from the base of the window. Where the paint finish becomes defective this may allow rot to become established. Small areas affected by rot may be filled with decorating fillers, but, where the amount of it is more serious, then it may be necessary to splice new pieces of timber into the existing members. The most important criterion is to try to reduce the amount of the original timber lost, as this will usually be more durable and better seasoned than any modern timber replacement.

Decorating Doors and Windows

Doors and windows have invariably been treated with modern oil gloss paints in the recent past, which do not allow the underlying timber to breathe. Provided that the area is not damp, this may not cause problems on internal joinery. However, where damp may be present this may cause the timber to rot, if the cause of the dampness is not dealt with. Earlier layers of more breathable paints such as lead-based ones are usually still present on original doors and windows. This means that additional health and safety precautions will be necessary when they are being prepared for redecoration. In addition, the use of blowlamps should be avoided as they are a fire hazard when used on an existing house. Where possible, try to redecorate doors and walls by using vapour-permeable paints (*see* Chapter 2) so that they allow the underlying surfaces to breathe. Environmentally-friendly paints that are water-based are a current option, but check their specification to ensure that they are also vapour-permeable or breathable. Also try to restrict the use of paints that have high levels of volatile organic compounds (VOCs) in them as they may contribute to air pollution. When rubbing down windows, be careful that the glass is not scratched since older glass tends to be slightly softer than modern glass. Old glass has a more rippled appearance, if looked at carefully, by comparison with modern glass, and so replacing it would mean that a part of the character of the house would be lost. Modern glass can be particularly noticeable among older glass by its different reflections as seen from the outside. When painting the interior of a sash window, make sure that the sash guide channels and the cords are free of paint as they could make it much more difficult to open and close the window. Also be careful to leave all windows slightly open after they have been painted so that they do not get sealed up in the closed position (*also see* Chapter 3).

Doors like this were never intended to have their paint removed as their softwood timber had knots in it (where the branches had started to develop) and were regarded as inferior. The sap often leaks out of a knot, even after many years, which is why a sealer known as 'knotting compound' was used to cover these areas and before the door was painted, to prevent the sap from damaging the paint finish.

FIREPLACES AND STOVES

Fireplaces were the most significant feature in the main living areas, but they were also the most likely ones to be replaced when fashions changed. Marble was popular for fire surrounds and was often white in living or reception rooms and black or a darker colour in dining rooms. Slate was often used instead and sometimes was painted or veined to look like marble. Cast iron was also popular during this period and many highly decorated designs were often incorporated into the mouldings. Other materials that may also be found are timber and stone. The inner part of the fireplace where the coals were placed was frequently made of cast iron to resist the heat. However, where the whole fireplace was made of cast iron a vertical row of decorative tiles on either side of the grate was also a popular feature, which additionally helped to reflect the heat. Kitchen ranges, which were the predecessors of the modern cooker, will have usually been removed, but the impression of a larger opening may still be faintly visible on the wall around a later stove or fireplace. More recently, back-boilers, or later, wood-burning stoves are now often placed in these locations.

Reinstating Missing Fire Surrounds

Where a fire surround is completely missing the alternatives are to have a new one made to a contemporary design or to reinstate a replica that is appropriate to the date of the house. When considering a new design it should be appropriate in style and proportion to the room for which it is intended. As a guide, reception rooms had more decorative fireplaces than bedrooms, where the designs were usually much simpler. There was a convention for white fire surrounds in drawing rooms and other 'feminine' rooms and black in dining rooms and 'masculine' rooms. Try to avoid buying salvaged fireplaces as they

ABOVE: This white marble fire surround has a curved opening with a cast-iron grate.

LEFT: This is a typical cast-iron insert for a fireplace in the earlier part of this period. The circular plate at the rear of the fireplace is pivoted at the bottom and has to be pushed backwards into the open position when the fire is to be used. Keeping this plate closed in winter, if the fire is unlit, is likely to reduce the amount of heat escaping up the flue. However, in summer it is advisable to push this plate into the open position to allow the room and the flue to be naturally ventilated. Where these circular plates are missing, new ones may be made to match or a second-hand one might be found. However, as the plates vary in size, to find one that fits exactly may be time-consuming. An interesting feature on this grate is the pin to the right; this would have been used to attach a swinging grid to heat water, for example.

ABOVE: A marble fire surround with tiles on either side of the cast-iron grate.

RIGHT: This cast-iron fireplace may have been painted with various colours many times in its history; the hearth may have been covered over or lost and that would need to be reinstated and the chimney cleaned and checked before the fireplace were ever reused.

These fireplaces are in adjoining groundfloor rooms connected by double doors. They are both black slate fire surrounds that have been decorated to resemble white marble. Where the paint finish has been damaged on the right side the slate is visible. The circular roundels on the brackets below the mantelshelf are missing and the three vertical groves at the bottom of the brackets have been covered. On the left side of the surround the outline of a rectangular decorative pattern, popular on slate fireplaces, is visible as in the next illustration (overleaf).

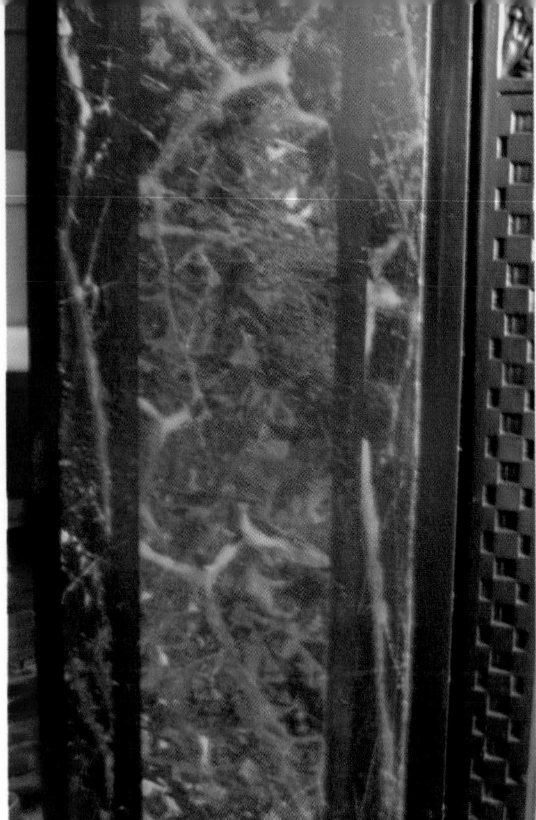

ABOVE: A detail of the decorative finish to the slate fire surround in the illustration on the left.

LEFT: A slate fire surround with decorative rectangular panels in a reception room.

are likely to have been removed from another house, which has therefore been deprived of its original fireplace. Where a later fireplace has been installed, consider keeping this as it explains the history and development of the house for future historians. For example, many replacement twentieth-century fireplaces are still being removed to make way for new ones. In a few years' time, when mid-twentieth-century fire surrounds may become fashionable once more, they are likely to be scarce and therefore historically valuable since so few survive. Old fireplaces may have previously been disposed of somewhere around the house or garden. This is because they were heavy and bulky items to remove before skips became popular later in the last century. Good places to search for old fireplaces are in the floor voids under existing timber floorboards or in out-of-the-way places, such as cellars or buried in the garden. As fireplaces are often constructed from a number of smaller elements, even if they have been broken up, it may be possible to reassemble them and put them back in place.

Repairs to Fireplaces

The types of repair depend on the material that the fireplace is made of and the extent of the damage it may have suffered. Some things may be better left as found and accepted as part of the history. Where, for example, a slate or marble fire surround has acquired marks as a result of wear and tear, these are a part of the on-going history. In trying to remove such marks one may draw more attention to them. Where tiles have been used for the hearth they are often damaged through being in constant use and form an historical record. Where hearth tiles are cracked or damaged it is usually best to leave them as they are, as it is virtually impossible to obtain exactly matching new ones and it also destroys some of the history. Where tiles have been chipped or cracked and the damage is noticeable it may be possible to conceal the damage by painting it with matching artists' paints. But usually the best option is to leave it as it was found so that it records the history and the development of the house.

This fireplace has many crisp details as it has not been repainted over the years.

Decorations to Previously Painted Fire Surrounds

Each time a previously painted fire surround is redecorated the additional layers of paint are likely to reduce the sharpness of the existing details. This applies particularly to cast-iron fire surrounds that usually have quite intricate details. However, removing paint from a fire surround destroys the record of the historical paint colours, and the removal of paint is also likely to make the surround look out of keeping with the rest of the house. This is because the details may become too crisp by comparison with

In this case a kitchen range has been removed and a mid-twentieth-century fireplace has been fitted into a reduced size of opening. The date of this alteration can be determined from the date of the 'new' design of fireplace.

the surroundings that have many layers of paint on them. In addition, lead-based paints may have been used in the past and these require additional precautions (*see* websites). Where the paint has been chipped earlier colours may be revealed and these may help in the choice of new colour schemes for the room. Where the fire surround is bare iron use a black metal grate polish to revive the original finish.

Ventilation of Chimney Flues

When fireplaces were not in use the Victorians often covered the openings with chimney boards to conceal them and to reduce draughts. Some fireplaces may have plates that close over the flue when not in use; however, these are a useful source of ventilation during the summer if left open. Try to avoid sealing up fireplaces and their flues completely as they need a throughput of air to allow any damp that gets into the chimney to escape. This is why airbricks, or some kind of permanent ventilator, are usually seen where the fireplace has been completely removed. Where a chimney is no longer in use, a ventilated chimney cap can be fitted over the top of it to reduce the amount of rain getting into the flue. These caps also reduce the draughts in the flue, as well as deterring birds from nesting in the chimney pot. They must be removed if a fireplace is to be reused.

Gas Coal-effect Fires and Stoves

Before proceeding with the installation of gas coal-effect fires or new stoves, think carefully about the implications and upheaval involved with such an installation. This is because both these types of installation usually cause a considerable amount of disruption to the house since flues usually have to be lined to comply with building regulations/standards (*see* websites). The easier type of flue liner to install is usually the flexible, stainless steel one, while rigid section liners are usually much more difficult to fit into an existing flue. For structural reasons, it may be worth trying to avoid the flue liners formed by

This stone fire surround and cast-iron grate have previously been painted and some of the paint on the inner iron part would probably not withstand the heat if the fire were to be reinstated; in addition, the hearth would also need to be reinstated.

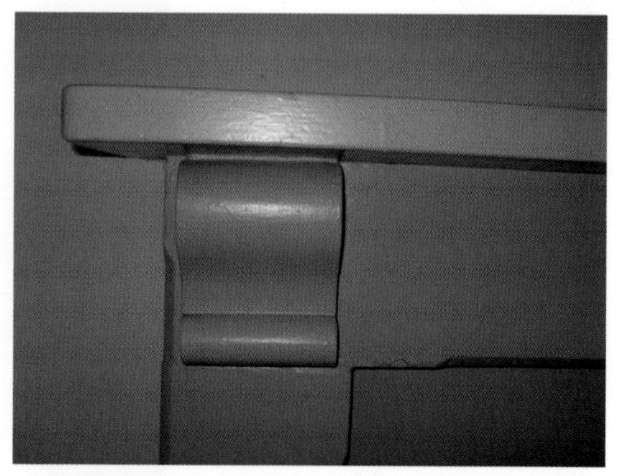

This stone fire surround has many layers of paint on it and it may be better to preserve this rather than try to remove the paint. If a more decorative finish or a different colour were required, this is much easier and less damaging to the history of the house than to try to remove the paint.

pouring a lining material down the chimney and around a former, and allowing it to set. This is because such a solid mass may not necessarily be compatible with the way an old house moves and breathes. A new gas fire requires a supply pipe and this can cause considerable disruption when being laid to reach the fireplace. In addition, where an open gas fire is installed a permanent air vent is legally necessary in the room to supply air to the fire and avoid the dangers of suffocation from a build-up of fumes or a lack of oxygen.

STAIRCASES

The staircase in the entrance hall is usually treated as a significant architectural feature in a Victorian or Edwardian home. The beginning of the handrail often has decorative features, such as curved ends or ornate newel posts (that secure the handrail in place at the beginning of the staircase). The handrail was commonly a natural wood finish, often a dark hardwood, as it would wear more gracefully than paint and, possibly, paint was avoided because the risks of regularly touching lead paint were understood. In some cases ornate, cast-iron columns were used to fix the handrail to the stair structure for additional stability. The stair treads were usually of timber but other materials such as stone may have been used between the basement and the first floor in certain types of house. Where stone was used the balusters were often of cast or wrought iron (*see* Chapter 5). On upper floors where the steps changed to timber, the balustrades may also have changed from metal to timber to match. At the beginning of the stair the area under them usually incorporated a cupboard. This was often enclosed with vertical timber boarding or panelling, depending on the style of the house. Where there is a cellar, the access door was usually incorporated into the end of this panelling. Over the years, the sides of the stair treads and balusters are likely to have been grained or painted in a variety of colours which may be visible when the paint has been chipped.

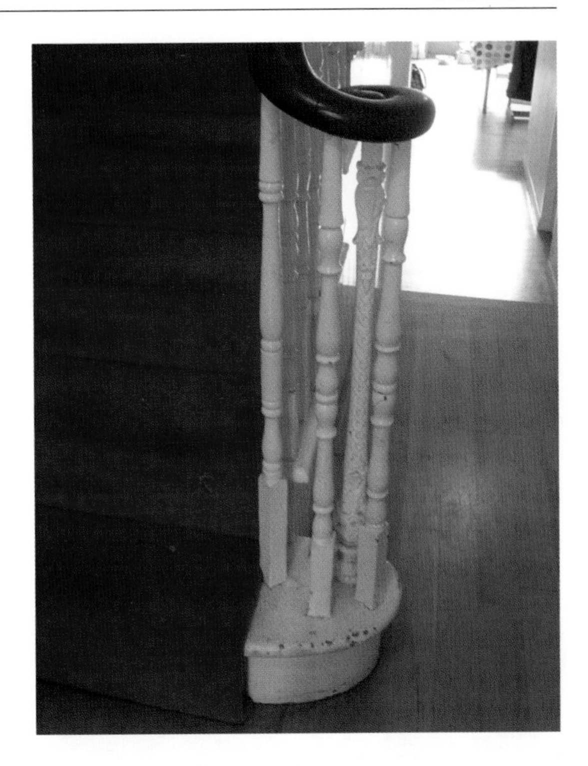

These turned timber balusters and handrails are reinforced by a cast-iron post at the end of the handrail, of a slightly different design from the balusters.

This newel post is an impressive feature in this entrance hall.

Repairs to Staircases

Where the projecting edges of a horizontal stair tread, known as a 'nosing', have worn away over time,

ABOVE: Earlier decoration schemes often favoured the balusters' matching the natural colour of the timber handrail. Lighter colours are now more popular, but try where possible to avoid painting the natural wood handrail or painting the earlier decorative graining of the balusters to preserve the history of them. At the rear of this staircase the original dado rail is visible on the landing below.

ABOVE RIGHT: The sides of understairs cupboards were often constructed from vertical timber boarding with a bead moulding to the edge of each board. Access to the cellar may have also have been from this area.

RIGHT: Here is a detail of the stair edge and timber moulding, with the vertical timber panelling of the understairs cupboard below.

simple repairs with timber spliced into the front of the tread may be carried out if necessary. Where a timber staircase has become damp, make sure that the source of it has been identified and that the area is thoroughly ventilated so that it dries out, which may take anything up to six months. The most vulnerable staircase is usually the one to the cellar, since a lack of ventilation is often the precursor to damp causing decay at the base of it. This can become a more serious structural problem if the staircase is allowed to remain damp as its structural integrity may be compromised.

Decorations

Generally, staircases are likely to have been painted many times over the years. Decorative paint effects that resemble graining may have been used to cover lighter colours, but where possible retain any earlier paint finishes since each time mouldings are repainted or rubbed down they lose some of their original crispness. Try to avoid painting handrails since here natural timber was usually displayed. Also try to avoid sanding them down as the patina of age is likely to be destroyed in the process. Where original or earlier graining remains on the balusters or the sides of stairs try to retain this increasingly rare finish as they are likely to have often been painted. As with redecorating other timber elements within the house, use breathable paints where this is reasonable and possible (*see* Chapter 2).

TIMBER MOULDINGS

There were various timber features used for decoration in houses of this date; however, the type and style were related to the original construction costs of the house. The three most common such features that may still exist are picture and dado rails and skirting boards. Picture rails were fixed at high level around the room so that pictures could easily be hung, as it was more difficult to fix picture hooks to lath and plaster walls. As their popularity went in and out of fashion over the years, they may have been removed at some time, although their impressions may still be visible where they were positioned. Dado rails are usually found around chair-back height on walls in areas that were subject to high wear and tear,

The underside of an entrance hall staircase, as seen from the steps down to the cellar.

This newel post has been reused to form the access to a loft extension, as indicated by the piecing in of timber to where a previous handrail would have been jointed into it.

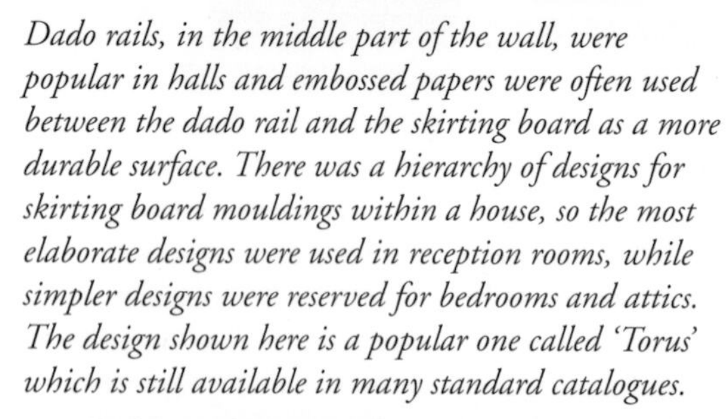

Dado rails, in the middle part of the wall, were popular in halls and embossed papers were often used between the dado rail and the skirting board as a more durable surface. There was a hierarchy of designs for skirting board mouldings within a house, so the most elaborate designs were used in reception rooms, while simpler designs were reserved for bedrooms and attics. The design shown here is a popular one called 'Torus' which is still available in many standard catalogues.

A close up of a 'Torus' skirting moulding.

Picture rails were usually found in most rooms as pictures were an easily portable form of decoration; this suited houses that were rented during this period. As picture hooks are not easily fixed into lath and plaster walls, this was a more versatile way of hanging pictures.

such as halls, landings and staircases. They were used as a decorative feature to divide up the wall visually, but they also had a practical purpose as a different type of wall finish may have been used below the rail that was more hardwearing or less likely to bring a chalky distemper into contact with clothing. Skirting boards were used to cover the junction between floors and walls. The elaborateness or otherwise of these three elements much depended on the function or status of the room or area within which they were being used and the style and design of the house.

Repairs to Timber Mouldings

Any of these features may be damaged through general wear and tear, but probably the most likely cause was prolonged dampness, as this is likely to rot the timber. First establish what is making the area damp and deal with the causes (see Chapter 2). Once this has been solved, allow the timber to dry out by ensuring plenty of through ventilation. This process may take several months. Only when the area is completely dry should the item be carefully examined to establish whether any repairs are actually necessary. The extent of any repairs usually depends on whether the item is structural or purely decorative. A small area of decay may be filled with decorating-type fillers, while a more seriously rotten area may require new timber to be spliced in. As it is usually difficult to find standard mouldings to exactly match the existing ones, try wherever possible to retain the original mouldings so that they may then be spliced on to any new pieces of timber. When painting timber pay particular attention to the type of paint to be used as a breathable finish is often desirable (*see* Chapter 2).

FLOORS

Most houses had both timber and solid floors, depending upon their location within the house. The majority of the floors would be of timber boards that were then covered with carpets, rugs, canvas floor cloths or sheet materials such as linoleum, depending on the function and use of the room. Generally, some entrance halls, service and cellar areas had solid floors as they were subject to heavier wear and tear and thus a solid one was more hardwearing in these situations. Solid floors tended to be finished with tiles, stone or timber parquet flooring in entrance halls, while more functional rooms, such as sculleries and cellars, would have quarry tiles or smooth floor finishes, such as a granolithic screed. Where there was a cellar under an entrance hall, the tiled finish was often laid on a screed supported on timber floor joists below.

This simple timber bead moulding covers a dropped beam over an opening.

This tiled floor is laid on a timber sub-floor.

Timber Floors

The majority of floorboards were generally not finished to a very high standard as they were usually covered in some manner. The only areas where they would have been on display were where the existing boards had been stained to a darker colour. This usually happens around the edges of rooms, where there may have been a central rug. Timber floorboards and joists need to be well ventilated as this reduces the possibility of damp getting in and rotting them. This is why most houses have air vents around the exterior of the house at low level to air the underfloor spaces. For this reason it is important that these vents are not blocked up as otherwise the floor timbers may become damp. The first signs of damp problems are usually a musty smell or the floorboards starting to feel soft underfoot. One way to deal with this is to lift individual floorboards at opposite ends of the room to allow through ventilation. In addition, check that the vents are functioning properly. A timber floor may take several months to dry out satisfactorily and it is only once the area is significantly dryer that the extent of any repairs may be established.

The most vulnerable places are usually where the floor joists are in contact with the external walls. If a metal point can be pushed into the timber by a significant amount, then repairs may be appropriate by splicing in new pieces of timber to the ends of the joists or by plating them with timber or metal. Metal plates usually cause less disruption than splicing in new pieces of timber. Where floorboards have started to rot, new lengths of board may be pieced in to match the existing ones. Where floorboards have shrunk to such an extent that the gaps between the boards are felt to be excessive, a material such as papier mâché or cork, which are both relatively breathable materials, may be used to fill them. Where the spaces are particularly large, thin fillets of timber may be used to fill the space between the boards, as appropriate. Try to avoid lifting the boards and moving them closer together to reduce the gaps; this is because a high proportion of boards may split where they have been nailed into place.

As carpets, rugs or other floor finishes may have originally been used to cover floorboards, the quality of the timber used was not particularly high. For this reason it is not sensible to sand the floors as the boards will never look very presentable. Furthermore, sanding irreversibly removes part of the surface of the boards. Leaving timber floors uncovered reduces the amount of thermal insulation to the floor and may contribute to noise levels in the house. Where carpets or underlays are laid, make sure that they are breathable so that air can circulate around the floorboards and the floor voids. Foam or rubber-backed carpets and underlays are not so breathable and do not allow air to circulate freely. Laminate floors that are placed over existing timber floors have recently been popular, but they restrict the breathability of the floorboards underneath. Adding another layer to an existing floor alters the detailing that is required at the junction with the existing elements, such as skirting boards, thresholds and fire surrounds, and the solutions may often look unresolved.

Floor Finishes

As many houses were rented rather than owned during this period, floor finishes such as rugs were popular as they were removable. Where a room has previously had a rug in it, the floorboards around the edges of the room may have been stained a darker colour. Where rugs are being reintroduced make sure that any underlay is of a breathable material. Fitted carpets are stretched over carpet grippers that are placed around the perimeter of a room, but as these have to be securely fixed into the floor, try to avoid their use where there is an original floor finish as the fixings are likely to damage it. Carpet grippers are convenient but not absolutely necessary. A margin was traditionally left on either side of a stair carpet or runner so that stair rods, often of brass, could be fixed to the timber stair on either side of the carpet. Stair carpets were made in standard widths, whereas the widths of staircases varied. The area between the carpet and the balusters was often stained, but later it may have been painted a lighter colour. With the arrival of fitted carpets there was less reliance on special stairwidth carpets and their width could be increased as necessary for each house.

Linoleum was a popular floor covering, made of cork and linseed oil and still available today. Early examples are now rare as it wears after a while. Old

A border to a stair carpet gives it emphasis. Metal stair-rods were traditional before carpet grippers were used, as here.

'lino' may be found under later layers of flooring. If areas of lino are found this is a valuable survival. Original patterns may still be matched and the material is considered to be a relatively environmentally-friendly product.

Tiled Floors

There were many popular and standard designs used throughout this period for entrance halls as well as paths to the house. A typical design used a combination of single coloured tiles, known as geometric tiles, with usually a smaller number of encaustic, multi-coloured, tiles as these were more expensive to produce. Encaustic tiles are made by at least two colours being used within a single tile. One design was pressed into the clay base and then a second, liquid colour was run into the resulting depression left by it. To support these tiles, they have to be laid on a solid base so that they do not crack. This base was usually laid on top of timber shuttering, if supported on timber floor joists. Tiles may start to crack where the supporting structure underneath a floor is inadvertently removed or decays; for example, in the cellar underneath one of these floors. Try to avoid lifting tiles because more damage is likely to occur in the process. If there is damage that attracts attention, this may be disguised by applying artists' paints to camouflage it. These types of floor were often covered over when they went out of fashion and the difficulty of removing later floor coverings depends on how well a later finish has bonded to the existing tiles. Most later finishes are removable, but expect that there may be some remaining damage or residue left on the tiles that is too difficult to remove without significantly damaging the tiles. Resist the temptation to apply a modern 'sealing' finish over the tiles as this is likely to seal in dampness that may lead to the long-term deterioration of the floor.

Stone and Marble Floors

Where stone or marble floors have been laid they are most likely to be damaged by damp getting into the surrounding structure. Try to avoid applying any sort of floor polish to them as this not only alters the character of the floor, but it may seal dampness into the floor and become a slip hazard as well. These types of floor are easily stained by water, so make sure

This design includes encaustic and geometric tiles. The former have at least two colours within each and are therefore more expensive to produce, whereas single-coloured geometric tiles were less expensive to manufacture and usually made up most of the design.

The design of this hall floor has been created from a combination of encaustic and geometric tiles and is laid on a solid base supported on timber floor joists.

Four colours are used for the design in this fragment of an encaustic tile.

The section of this tile shows the depth of the slips of coloured liquid clay that were used for making encaustic tiles.

that any dripping pipes are dealt with immediately. Removing stains is never easy and unlikely to be completely satisfactory, so avoid allowing any stains to happen in the first place. Where the floor has been chipped or damaged, it is possible to apply fillers that build up the missing areas to match, but make sure that no fillers contain non-reversible glues. Try to avoid lifting this type of floor as more damage is likely to occur in the process. Where stone has already been coated with an impervious finish, this may not be allowing the stone to breathe. This may be evident where the stone is beginning to deteriorate. If this is happening, then it may be appropriate to try and remove the existing finish to allow the stone to breathe. The removal of finishes from stone is not easy and often it may not be possible to completely remove them, if they have soaked into the stone.

Parquet Floors

Thicker parquet floors were usually made from solid pieces of hardwood or fine softwood that were laid in regular patterns in a liquid base of tar and pitch, and usually on solid ground floors. Thinner parquet floors, which had been popular from previous centuries, were more usually applied over timber boards and could have quite elaborate designs. They were a relatively expensive floor finish and so were used sparingly only in visible areas. An economic way of using parquet flooring was to lay it around the edges of a room, with cheaper floorboards in the central part that would be covered by a rug. Objects being dragged across timber floors may scratch them and stiletto-heeled shoes often leave an impression. Where individual parquet blocks start to lift, this may be a sign that there is a problem with the sub-floor, this may range from struts having been

This herringbone-patterned parquet floor of thick blocks was relaid where the existing one had been removed.

removed that were supporting the underside of the floor to a very dry atmosphere in which the blocks shrink and become loose.

Quarry Tiles

These are fairly robust clay tiles, which are generally square and were often used in areas of high wear and tear. They are most likely to be damaged by heavy objects being dropped on to them. Where the damage is significant enough to need to be repaired, try to avoid lifting adjacent, undamaged tiles as there are likely to be further breakages caused. In addition, it is usually difficult to find matching tiles. Quarry tiles do not respond well to being damp for long periods, they may, for example, exhibit staining from soluble salts or limescale, so make sure that any dampness in the surrounding fabric is dealt with. Repair any water pipe leaks before they create more extensive damage to the floor itself. As with other tiled finishes, try to avoid applying impervious finishes, such as waxes or polishes, to them as these may create more problems and become a slip hazard.

Granolithic Floor Finishes

This was a popular finish that was applied in areas that had a high level of traffic, such as sculleries, service areas or cellars. It was a hardwearing screed of cement mixed with granite or other chippings to give it abrasion-resistance or non-slip qualities. It was laid as a fairly stiff 'liquid' and so could be laid to a fall for drainage purposes if required.

Caring for Solid Floors

Where possible, try to avoid the floors being scratched. To reduce the amount of grit that can get on to the floor, try to position doormats carefully so that they remove grit from shoes before it scratches the floor. But make sure that the mat does not have a rubber back as this may cause problems if the floor underneath is not allowed to breathe. Cleaning solid floors with a vacuum cleaner is preferable to sweeping them as this lifts grit away from the surface rather than dragging it over the surface. However, rollers on the bottom of a vacuum cleaner may also damage the floor. Try to avoid any aggressive water cleaning or the use of abrasives on these types of floor as they are likely to cause more damage in the process. Sealers or varnishes should be avoided as they reduce the ability of the floor to breathe and that, in turn, reduces the ability of any dampness within the floor to escape and this may lead to the deterioration of the surface finish.

Furnishings

To find original curtains and fabrics in a house is fairly rare as they are usually one of the first items to be changed by new owners, if they have not already been removed. There may be hints as to how certain rooms were furnished from the clues that remain. For example, where roller blinds have been used in the past for shading the interiors, the ends of the blind mechanisms may still remain. The fixing positions of curtain rails may also still be visible under later layers of paint or paper. Where a house still retains more

Historically inspired designs from the date of the house may be a starting point for an interior decoration scheme. It is sensible to fit curtains with thermal linings to retain heat within the room when the curtains are closed.

Even such things as blinds can have thermal linings incorporated into them, as in this case.

recent fabrics and furnishings they are also a part of the house's history. Where any new curtains are being made to fit the existing windows ensure that they include thermal linings to retain heat within the rooms. Fitting pelmets over the tops of the curtains will also help. In addition, look at Victorian and Edwardian photographs for inspiration as to the types of curtain that might be appropriate to use.

Furniture

Furniture that is contemporary with the age of the house is often easier to get in and out of it as it was usually divisible into smaller sections for ease of moving. Many items of furniture were designed with the proportions of Victorian and Edwardian houses in mind. For example, freestanding wardrobes were designed to fit within the alcoves at the sides of bedroom fireplaces, and the height of such furniture often relates to the height of picture rails. Furniture from this period was typically of dark wood or varnished in imitation of dark woods. This would have matched the grained and varnished doors, windows and timber joinery that were popular during parts of our period. Buying secondhand furniture also means that less energy is expended in making new. When bringing old furniture into a house, check it over for signs of active woodworm as this would indicate that it might have been previously kept in a damper environment. Woodworm should eventually disappear once the moisture content in the furniture is reduced.

Where upholstered furniture is being considered for reupholstering, consider how much of the original may be retained, as it is often parts such as

The proportions of furniture contemporary with the date of the house are usually suited to its spaces.

Using picture rails to hang pictures was the traditional way to display pictures and allowed for them to be changed around more easily.

webbing that have broken and that may easily be repaired. Where a piece of furniture is completely reupholstered and new upholstery materials used its history is lost, so try to reuse as much of the existing upholstery materials as possible. Where the top layer of fabric has been damaged this might possibly be reupholstered without disturbing the underlying layers. Alternatively, loose covers may be made to fit which can be removed and cleaned as and when necessary.

Accessories

As many Victorian and Edwardian houses were rented rather than owned, the comfort of the home was created by portable decorations. Pictures are probably the most obvious example of this as they are able to make a significant difference to the setting of a room.

SERVICES

In order for houses to function to modern day standards, they now require various services to be brought into them and others to take waste away. Since many of these houses were built before these services were commonly available, they have often been adapted over the years to accommodate them. Services now incorporated into houses are usually running water for kitchens and bathrooms and electricity, that replaced oil lamps or town gas, for lighting. The drains that remove waste from internal WCs may either be separately piped away from the house or, in some situations, they may have been combined with the rainwater disposal system into a single drainage connection to the main sewer. Threading these newly available services into the existing fabric usually meant that they were more visible as they were not fully integrated into the original design of the house. Where services are to be altered or introduced into a house now, the installers have to be qualified to prescribed standards (*see* websites).

Electrics

Early electrical wiring was, like gas and water pipes, often attached to the surface of a wall, while most electrical wiring is now usually concealed either within floor and ceiling voids or between lath and plaster partitions. Where the walls are of solid masonry construction, they may have been chased to fit new cables. The routes of these chases are usually visible as it is generally quite difficult to conceal them well. Where new electrical fittings are being proposed these should be sited as close as possible to existing cable runs to reduce further disruption to the fabric of the house. Faults in electrical wiring are a fire hazard, so it is a sensible precaution to get a qualified electrician (*see* websites) to test the system.

Work on an existing system now has to be carried out by a qualified electrician under current building regulations/standards (*see* websites). Where new cables are required, consider carefully where the routes are to be located to minimize the amount of chasing of walls or surface-mounted wiring that is necessary. Energy-efficient lamps are becoming available for an ever greater number of light fittings, so ensure that, when existing bulbs fail, they are replaced with energy-efficient types. However, be aware that some dimmer switches and automatically-switched circuits do not work with energy-saving, compact fluorescent lamps. Some electrical fittings that are old enough to be interesting might not be adaptable to meet current regulations. But for posterity retain these where possible in the room in which they were found, or fix them somewhere nearby as a historical record. Particular types of new dimmer light switch may require deeper recesses beneath the switch plate than the existing ones and may involve more disruption to fit them.

Consider the positioning of smoke detectors in relation to other elements of the surrounding architecture; however, they need to be positioned where they are able to work properly and so cannot be hidden.

Security alarm systems often need to be incorporated into houses to increase levels of security. There are two types of system that may be considered. Those that use cables to connect the detectors to the main control panel inevitably involve a considerable amount of upheaval. This is because the walls often have to be chased to accommodate the cables; otherwise surface-mounted cables are not particularly attractive. The other type of security system now available is a wireless system. These are more sympathetic to older houses as they do not require walls to be chased because the detectors are connected by radio waves. With any security system, consider the location of the control panel and the design of the fittings so that they are as unobtrusive as possible. Smoke detectors should be installed, if they are not already present. But when installing them consider carefully how the positioning of the detectors relates to architectural features, such as cornices and light fittings, as well as positioning them to function correctly.

Lighting

Rarely are many earlier light fittings found because when the wiring is updated the fittings are also usually changed. The proportions and style of new light fittings should be in keeping with the area to be illuminated. There are many reproduction lampshades available as well as contemporary light fittings; so the choice depends on the general style of the particular room or area. There are a great variety of electrical switch plates now available, but consider whether any of the existing fittings are historic examples. They may not be usable if they do not meet current regulations, but they are an interesting part of the history and should be kept in the house for this reason. Where table or freestanding light fittings are being used there are many colours of plastic or fabric-covered flex now available which can be used to disguise the cables more discreetly than the standard white plastic type.

Telephone Cables

Where new installations or existing wiring is being updated be careful to ensure that the cables are not fixed to any architectural features. Often, with some forward planning about where cables are being routed, they can be discreetly hidden.

Gas

Gas supply pipes to new fittings such as fires may be difficult to route through an existing house without their being visible. Once gas appliances have been installed, a sensible precaution is to have carbon monoxide detectors fitted in the house. Registered gas fitters are required to deal with gas appliances (*see* websites).

Open Fires

Heating a house by using open fires was the most popular form of heating before the advent of central heating. By Victorian times coal was widely available, so most houses were equiped with the smaller, coal-burning grates. There are restrictions about the types of fuel that can be used in certain locations, so check whether the local area is a smokeless zone (*see* websites). Where fires are in use the flues should be regularly swept, particularly at the beginning of the winter, to avoid a potential build-up of soot and to ensure that birds have not nested in the chimney during the summer.

The 'stalk' projecting from the centre of this ceiling rose remains from the pipe for an early town-gas light fitting and is a part of the historical record of the house.

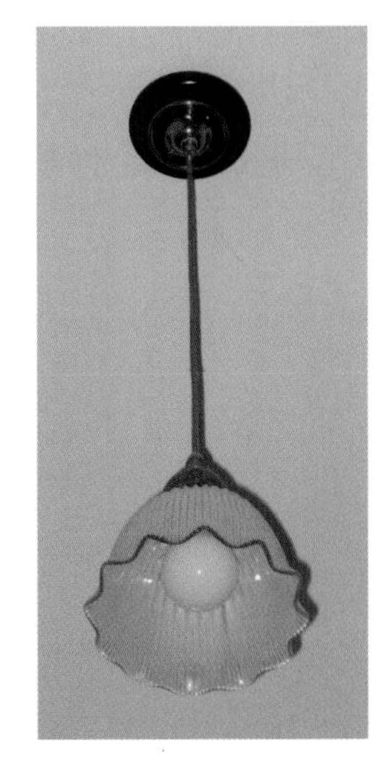

Simple and elegant light fittings are timeless and to which low-energy lamps can usually be fitted.

Plumbing

Where original iron or lead plumbing pipes still remain these are a part of the history of the house and, wherever possible, they should be retained. Many types of earlier plumbing are often carefully handcrafted pieces of work that are of increasing interest so these too should be retained. There are, however, safety issues about lead plumbing on domestic drinking water supplies (see Websites).

Heating Pipes and Radiators

Where there is an existing heating system, it will have been installed with valves at each radiator. To employ the existing heating system as efficiently as possible, use the valves to turn radiators on or off, depending on the occupancy of a room at any particular time. Where there are early or original radiators, rather than replace them, consider using additional means of heating as required to supplement the existing system, which may be of historical interest in itself. Where a house is listed, the listing will cover original and later radiators, as well as all other interior features. Where either new or additional pipes are being added to a heating system, care should be taken not to notch or drill holes through floor joists as this is likely to weaken them. Where there are old pipes that have earlier forms of lagging around them be

Where old radiators and pipework exist they are a part of the house's history and, where a house is listed, they are automatically covered by the listing.

aware that this may contain asbestos, so having the material tested is a sensible precaution (*see* websites). There are many reproduction radiators that are now available that can be incorporated into new or existing heating systems to suit the style of the interior.

All pipes in unheated areas should be lagged to conserve heat and reduce the likelihood of frost damage.

Cooking Ranges

Victorian and Edwardian houses usually had a coal-fired kitchen range that was used for cooking. This usually meant that coal storage was a necessary part of most houses to keep the ranges functioning. Modern cookers are now usually powered by gas or electricity, although some larger twentieth-century ranges were often oil-fired. Liquid propane gas is also an option in rural areas where gas is not available. However, both oil and propane require storage tanks and easy access for delivery lorries. Some types of kitchen range that remain on all the time consume large quantities of fuel and may not be such an environmentally-friendly or economical option.

Underfloor Heating

This is currently popular, but as this type of system usually has to be laid in a solid base or requires the raising of existing timber floor levels, there is often a conflict in trying to fit them into an older house, where the solid floors may first need to be excavated or where existing timber floors may be disturbed. Where underfloor heating has been installed it is inadvisable to lay carpets over these systems as this will reduce the amount of heat that is transferred into the room.

Hot and Cold Water Pipes

Hot and cold water pipes are often surface-mounted and, while they may not be things of beauty while they are on display, more leaks are more likely to be noticed than when they are concealed within boxing. Where pipes run through unheated areas, such as roof spaces or below floors, they should be lagged as a precaution against frost damage. Where old pipes have previously been lagged they might contain asbestos, so have this material analysed as a precaution (*see* websites). Where the plumbing is contemporary with the house, the cold-water tap in the kitchen would ordinarily have been connected direct to the main water supply. The cold water intended for a hot water cylinder often comes from an attic storage tank, sometimes this feeds WC cisterns and even basin taps as well. As the majority of domestic water pipes were originally made from lead, drinking water can be tested to establish its safety, should lead pipes be suspected (*see* websites). With an old house it is worth establishing which cold taps are delivering drinking water and which are fed by a storage tank.

Water Storage Tanks

It is sensible to lag water tanks to avoid the potential for them to freeze and then start to leak. Avoiding lagging directly under storage tanks means that they could get some residual heat from the room below to keep the temperature above freezing.

Plumbing Leaks

These are often not discovered until they have done considerable amounts of unseen damage. A typical problem is that a radiator pipe leaks and then the water starts to rot the timber laths of the ceiling below, and it may not be until quite a time afterwards that this is realized. Be vigilant and always investigate any leaks as soon as they are noticed.

If water gets into a lath and plaster ceiling from a plumbing leak, as here, make sure that the floorboards are lifted to allow the timber to dry out and then have the ceiling examined to see whether the laths or plaster needs like for like repair or reinforcement.

Floods

Cellars are usually the first areas to be flooded. Precautions such as running any new electrical wiring routes at high level to avoid their getting wet are sensible precautions. Cross ventilation is important in cellars to keep timberwork dry, so ensure that it is able to dry out naturally rather than introduce additional forms of heating to artificially dry it out. Lift a number of floorboards at opposite ends of rooms to allow for cross ventilation of underfloor voids. Where possible, remove damp material to allow for the whole area to dry out as naturally as possible. While pumps may be an option to install in cellars, they may be able to cope with only small amounts of water and in some situations its continual throughput may draw the mortar out of the walls.

FIRE PRECAUTIONS

- Make sure that the electrical wiring has been tested by a qualified electrician (see websites) and that all appliances are switched off when not in use.
- Avoid the use of inset downlighters in ceilings for both fire and sound insulation reasons (see earlier in this chapter).
- Make sure that gas appliances are checked on a regular basis by a properly registered installer (see websites). In rented properties, gas appliances have to be checked annually. In addition, buy a carbon monoxide detector.
- Be cautious about the use of wood-burning stoves, especially in thatched properties as the temperatures that may be reached in flue pipes may be considerable and make sure that no fuel is stacked up close to the stove.
- If the house does not already have smoke detectors make sure that they are fitted immediately and kept in good order.
- If any existing internal doors have door closers already fitted to them, this is likely to be in connection with protecting the means of escape from upper floors in case of fire. Make sure that these doors are not obstructed from closing at any time; otherwise the fire protection is likely to be reduced.
- Make sure that fire blankets and fire extinguishers are located in kitchens and other high-risk areas.
- In some areas, the fire service may offer to advise householders on fire safety in their homes.

CHAPTER 5

Setting

The setting of the house is important to create a pleasant environment. Take a careful look at the house from further away, as this is likely to give a good overview of it in its local setting. Taking pictures may also help, as they put the house and its relationship to any nearby buildings into perspective. Often it may be only minor things that have been changed in the past, but these may have a considerable impact not only on the house itself but also on those that surround it. This is why local authorities usually now have guidelines on their websites as to how the environment around houses in an area should be looked after.

BOUNDARY WALLS

Where a group of houses were built at around the same time, the boundary walls were usually fairly similar. However, subsequent owners may have made alterations over the years. Where a house forms part of a group of similar houses, ideally it is better if the boundary walls are treated in the same way. Where walls were used in preference to full-height railings, the local building materials most readily available were often used. Bricks or stones that were left over from the building of the house or that were rejected for use in the house walls were often recycled in the

The surroundings of the house contribute to its character.

The garden and the boundary walls enhance the setting of this Victorian villa.

garden walls. These walls usually had gates and gateposts and the materials used again depended upon whatever was most easily available. Cast iron and timber were both popular. However, few timber gates have survived as they are more likely to have rotted over the years through poor maintenance. In areas where stone or slate were the local materials substantial pieces were often used for gateposts.

Where any original walls still remain try to do as little as possible to them. The most important criteria are to ensure that water is not allowed to get into the core of the wall and damage it. The careful repair of boundary walls is usually necessary only where there are obvious signs of problems that are making the wall unstable. The most important factor with boundary walls is to ensure that water is deflected away from them. Make sure that whatever features were used to protect the head of the wall are not letting water into its core. Where there are coping stones that protect the top check these to ensure that they are not cracked and that the mortar around them is undamaged. When the pointing is found to be deeply recessed or missing on the sides of walls this is probably the time at which to consider repointing small areas, but only as absolutely necessary.

Be wary of repointing the whole face of a wall as this often creates more problems than it solves and is usually unnecessary. Any new mortar mix should respect the original underlying mortar type (and not necessarily any other recent repointing). If the mortar is soft when it is scratched with a metal point, then it is most probably a lime and sand-based mix and may well be the original material; its softness is not necessarily an indication of failure (*see* Chapter 2). Lime mortars are often soft enough to scratch with a finger nail, which indicates that some water may soak in, but it can also dry out. However, if the mortar is very hard (and it may also have small hairline cracks in it),

Boundary walls can add interest to the setting.

Traditionally, houses from this date often have low boundary walls with privet hedges above.

Architectural features may often be mirrored in hedges around the house, as here, the arch-headed door is matched by the privet hedge.

then this is more likely to have already been repointed with a cement and sand mortar mix. Where a mortar is too hard, it can trap water, which can then cause frost damage or it can prevent the bricks and stones from moving and make them crack. As some walls were originally built with a cement-based mortar, which was a relatively new development during this period, take a close look at the pointing to see whether it looks as if it has been replaced or whether this might still be the original mortar.

Boundary walls are often adjacent to pavements.

These substantial stone gateposts make an imposing entry to this group of houses, so ensure that any gate hinge pins fixed to them are kept well painted where they are in contact with stone, because, if rust becomes established, when it expands it may start to split the stone.

Details like this carved house name add to the setting and presence of the house.

These are cast-iron railings and gates as the design is identically repetitive. To keep ironwork in good condition, it has to be kept well painted to avoid rust beginning, which, if not dealt with, may lead to costly repairs.

As paving is often made of a relatively impervious material, this means that any water that gets into the base of the wall may not be able to escape again on the public side of the wall. In these situations try to incorporate a breathing space, perhaps by using gravel, between the wall and any adjoining hard surface within the garden, to allow dampness from the base of the boundary wall to escape. Otherwise the trapped damp may lead to the deterioration of the wall just above pavement level. To ensure the long-term future of these walls, try to avoid planting any new trees or potentially large shrubs too close to them. Where there is ivy growing over a wall, it is a sensible precaution to remove it (*see* Chapter 2). Where a large amount of ivy is allowed to grow over the top of freestanding walls it may increase the wind resistance, as it is an evergreen plant. During high winds the ivy may be blown off the wall or, in some cases, take parts of the wall with it. Try to avoid placing new plants where earth has been allowed to build up against a wall, as damp may be trapped. Where this has happened soil might be lowered again to allow air to circulate to help dry the wall.

Metal Gates and Railings

Gates and railings are frequently made from either cast or wrought iron. The type of iron is usually determined from the design of the metal-

These are an unusual design for cast-iron railings.

A detail of the railings of the house above.

The empty pockets in the stone indicate where railings were previously removed. There is also shown here a useful gravel breathing space between the pavement and the wall.

The curving elements have been hammered out of wrought iron.

This gate is made from wrought iron because the scroll elements have been beaten into shape with a hammer and clamped together, rather than having been cast in one piece.

work. Wrought iron is beaten and hammered into shape while the iron is hot. This is in contrast to cast iron that is moulded when molten for use in more repetitive designs. Carved wooden patterns of the design are pressed into a damp sand mixture to form a mould into which liquid iron is poured. Wrought iron has an almost fibrous structure and is fairly resilient. By contrast, cast iron has a crystalline structure, can be brittle and so snaps fairly cleanly when broken. Sometimes gates or railings are made up from a combination of the two materials. Railings were either used as a feature by themselves or placed on top of low brick or stone walls. Many iron railings were removed as part of the war effort between 1939 and 1945, but were then found to be unsuitable for their intended uses.

Metal railings start to rust when the paint film on them is punctured and water gets in behind it and is trapped there by the surrounding paint. The weakest points are junctions, either between parts of the design or the railing fixing points. Where railings were fixed into stone plinths, the holes were lined with lead to create a waterproof junction. Where rust gets established at this junction the railings may split the plinth and cause further damage. The best form of maintenance is to keep the paint film intact. Where any rust becomes apparent it should be removed to expose the bare metal ready for repainting. Lead paints may have

ABOVE: These railings are made from cast iron. Missing pieces can be reinstated if their loss detracts from the overall design or reduces its structural integrity. When considering repairs the most important factor in this type of work is to find a repairer who fully understands the materials that they are working with and reuses rather than replaces them.

RIGHT: The cast-iron brace on this gate post cleverly doubles as a boot scraper.

been used on railings in the past and these require special precautions when they are being rubbed down (*see* websites). Repainting should be carried out on a regular basis with special metal primers on bare metal and can then be followed by micaceous iron oxide (MIO) paint, and that covered with a decorative coat of paint if desired. Thicker paints, like MIO, may tend to obscure fine details in the metalwork, so their use has to be balanced against the protection of the railings for the future.

Railings on top of a wall were a popular feature that was often combined with a hedge behind. Where railings are fixed direct into the coping stone on top of the wall, molten lead was poured into the hole around the railing to make the junction waterproof.

Where water has got under the paint finish at a joint the rail has begun to lift as it rusts. A red-coloured primer has been applied to the bare metal to halt further rusting before redecoration can take place.

Because this cast-iron railing has not been painted, water has not been trapped under any later paint surface that could cause it to rust. Cast iron can be surprisingly resistant to rust if fully exposed to the air.

Timber Gates and Gateposts

Gates and gateposts were often made of timber, and it is fortunate if the original wood has survived. If there are any original timber elements, it is probable that an impervious paint finish will have since been used on them. Provided that the paint film is continuous, this may not cause a problem. Where it has split and water is able to get in under the paint this will become trapped and then start to rot the timber. Earlier layers of paint may be lead-based so precautions are necessary when repainting older timberwork (see websites). Where there is still original timber, repairs using the minimum amount of new wood are most appropriate, historically and also practically if the original is of higher quality than modern timber.

Hedges, Walls and Railings

The combination of hedges and walls, in addition to railings, was a popular setting for the front boundary. The hedge was often of privet, a small leafed shrub. It introduces colour into urban areas and a row of privet bushes, where regularly pruned, is able to create a continuation of the wall above it that contributed to the privacy at the front of the house. These hedges have often recently been removed because they require to be cut several times a year. Old photographs of Victorian and Edwardian streets often show the uniformity that such hedges brought to individual streets.

Reinstating Lost Walls or Railings

Original, unaltered walls or railings may be rare, depending on the area. If you are considering reinstating a lost boundary, look at other houses around to establish what was usual. But be wary of assuming that a popular design is original, as one later design idea may have been used at several different houses but which may not be contemporary with the construction date of the house. Where a house is listed or in a conservation area consents may be required, even where original elements are being reinstated or sympathetic alterations are being considered, so consult the local conservation officer.

PATHS

Paths are often one of the few original features that are likely to remain as money and attention were often focused on the house. To establish whether an existing path is original, look at others in the locality. However, be aware that what may appear to be a popular design may not necessarily be an original design dating from the building of the house. Paths are relatively delicate. Tiles or stones may be damaged within a path when heavy objects are dropped on it, when furniture is being moved in or out of the house, by the installation of manholes and access covers, and when the base on which the tiles or stones are laid begins to be disturbed and the path starts to settle and crack, and if heavy objects such as plant pots are placed on the path these may in time compress its base. Try to avoid planting trees or large shrubs too close to paths as their roots may in the longer term disturb the base. So make sure that the path is adequately protected in these situations. Where there are missing tiles it may be difficult to find new ones that are a close match to the originals. In these situations it may be easier to repair them with lime mortar coloured to match the existing. However, the most important criterion is to try to avoid lifting the

The setting enhances the overall appearance of a house.

While the original black and while doorstep remains, the path and rope edging tiles are replacements. They are, however, part of the house's history.

Original tiled paths like this are increasingly rare.

This is a typical design for a path made from encaustic and geometric tiles. Encaustic tiles have several colours within an individual tile, while geometric tiles are made with only one colour.

Square tiles were also popular, but try to ensure that later additions such as manhole covers are positioned well away from such original features as this path.

These are two types of original path or lawn edging.

Original edgings may be discovered anywhere in a garden.

Reproduction rope edging tiles are now available, but be careful about selecting colours and materials that blend with the surroundings.

Only ever use non-abrasive cloths and a little water to clean tiles, if they are to be cleaned at all, since too much cleaning may increase natural wear or destroy the patina of age.

existing tiles since more are likely to be damaged in the process. If there is a good reason for lightly cleaning them, use only non-abrasive cloths and the minimum of water. In addition, try to avoid applying finishes to the tiles as these may lead to dampness being trapped within them and thus cause the tiles to deteriorate.

Reinstating Existing Paths

If you are considering reinstating an original path where it appears to be missing, take a careful look around the area to see what paving materials and designs were originally used. There is also the possibility that the original path may have been covered over because it was damaged, rather than because fashions changed. In this case repairs are likely to be necessary once the original surface has been uncovered. When considering reinstating an original design or making alterations to an existing path, such as replacing a non-original edging, be aware that however the path has been treated recently this is all a part of the house's history and its setting and any subsequent alterations may erase this history. Where a house is listed or in a conservation area, consents may be required, even when original elements are being reinstated or altered, so consult your conservation officer. Where one house forms part of a terrace

This original decorative pattern may have later additions in black and white tiles.

Entrance steps form part of the approach to a house.

or group, any alterations that are being considered should be examined within their setting. The reason for this is that groups of houses were often intended to be fairly uniform in character when they were built, so try to avoid making one house look more prominent than those that surround it.

ENTRANCE STAIRS

Many houses with a basement often have a flight of steps up to the front door. The walls on either side of this are often of masonry with a coping stone on top to protect the wall from the weather. In some cases there may have been cast-iron balusters and a handrail fixed into the coping stone or direct into the steps if there are no side walls. Where the handrails appear to be missing, look at other similar types of house to see whether theirs still remain. In addition, look for clues as to whether railings may have been removed in the past. There may be cases where the steps start to allow water to get into the area under the stairs that are often a habitable part of the house. Before considering any particular solution, take a careful look at what appears to be causing the problem. Damp usually gets into the fabric of the house only if it is unable to drain away, so check that the water is draining away freely. In addition, check that the pointing or the junctions between the steps are not allowing water to intrude. It may be only a very small area that is defective, but this may be allowing a considerable amount of water to enter. Carefully repair any defects and then wait several months to see whether the area has properly dried out before considering whether any additional work may be necessary.

RUBBISH AND RECYCLING BINS

Brightly coloured rubbish and recycling bins can have a significant visual impact on the setting of a house or a group of them, so try to locate these where they are least noticeable. This may involve screening them with plants grown on frameworks or within purpose-made enclosures to reduce their visual impact. Where a house is listed or in a conservation area permissions may be required so speak to the local authority.

PARKING SPACES

In recent years many front gardens have had their front walls removed to create parking spaces. Where a house forms part of a row or a group this can have a considerable, and often detrimental, visual impact. Furthermore, the introduction of areas of impervious materials and new gullies affects where rainwater is able to drain away. This can contribute to damp problems, deplete the water table and create a burden on the drains. Where a house is listed, in a conservation area or falls within other planning restrictions, permissions for these changes may be required.

Hard standings can affect the appearance and drainage of front gardens.

SERVICES

Where new services, such as gas or oil pipes or telecommunication cables, are being provided to the house, trenches may have to be dug, so make sure that any paths or original features do not have to be disturbed. Where there are trees in the garden make sure that the route of any supplies does not run under their canopy as their roots may be damaged in the process and this could affect the health of the trees as well as subjecting the pipes or cables to future disturbance. Where a new oil tank is being considered this has to be carefully sited to comply with current regulations as well as being accessible for deliveries. Its location should be carefully considered in relation to the setting of the house and within the garden.

Hedges within front gardens add visual interest to the setting.

GARDENS

In order to understand an existing garden and how it functioned in relation to the house, start by looking at it to establish what historical planting and features still exist. While front gardens were often decorative, rear gardens were more functional. For example, a privy or earth closet was usually placed somewhere in the rear garden if it was not attached to the house. There may also be clues as to where ash pits were located or fuel storage areas, if the house does not have a cellar. Anything from old stone sinks to redundant coppers used for heating water might also be found in the garden. As skips have been available for only around a generation, unwanted items were previously recycled, buried or burnt before the ash was taken away by cart.

Alterations to the house and garden are often associated with a change of ownership, so establishing sale dates is helpful. Mature plants may be datable by variety as they were more likely to be planted when they were popular. Elder or yew trees were often planted near privies because they were thought to disguise smells or ward off flies, so they may still be growing in these locations long after the privy had been demolished. The height and girth of a tree, for its variety, are usually good indicators of its age. Unusual varieties of tree may be more closely dated to when they became popular. Where there were locally available materials these were often incorporated into the surrounding houses or gardens. For example, the waste material from a local foundry might have been used to make garden paths. Local archives may produce some interesting discoveries, as might internet searches and local studies libraries. Photographs of the fronts of houses and their gardens are the more likely to be tracked down as rear gardens were usually less accessible.

What may have existed in the past may much depend on the size, location and orientation of the garden. There may still be clues as to the original design from the current plants within it. Lawn edgings may be found buried in the grass or the remains of paths or paving materials may be uncovered. Look at nearby gardens to identify what features might be common in local gardens of around the same age. The existing plants and the local area are good indications of what suits the local environment and soil. Historical photographs of the area may help to identify particular plants that were popular in the past. Where considering adding new plants or shrubs, choose those that are unlikely to outgrow the space around them.

Outbuildings often reflect the history of how a house has evolved with time. If existing outbuildings are being considered for alteration or adaptation, the ideal basis of any alteration from a conservation point of view should be that the works will be completely reversible (*see* Chapter 2), so that the existing fabric is not damaged. Alterations to outbuildings are likely to require planning permission and, where a house is listed or in a conservation area – depending of the works proposed, consents may be required, so consult the local planning department.

TREES

Where parcels of land were developed to create Victorian and Edwardian streets, trees were often planted as part of the streetscape. There may be a hierarchy of the types of tree that were planted along the pavements in different streets. While the local council usually looks after these trees, they do contribute a valuable and useful part of the environment. Where trees are in the garden of a house, if it is within a conservation area, this means that an application has to be submitted to the local authority for approval before most types of works are carried out to the trees. In addition, particularly significant trees or groups of them may have individual tree preservation orders (TPOs) on them, so check this with the local authority.

Deciduous trees make a garden look very different between winter and summer, so experience the garden for at least a year to see how it currently works within the different seasons. In the past, trees may have been planted for a range of reasons – this may be to obscure unsightly views or to shade certain parts of the house or garden during the summer or to act as windbreaks. For these reasons be cautious about considering the pruning of any trees before the design of the whole garden has been fully understood throughout the seasons. Identifying the types of existing tree with a rough idea of age or maturity is a good starting point. The local authority's tree officer can be a useful point of contact. Trees have a natural life cycle and, when they are approaching their mature phase, consider what new trees may be planted in preparation for when older trees eventually die. When considering the planting of new trees make sure that they are appropriate in size and character to the setting, so that they do not outgrow it in time.

Trees can enhance the setting of a street.

Trees may either frame or obscure the architectural details of a house, so consider their long-term impact when they are being planted.

Keep a watchful eye on trees in the garden and those in the surrounding area. Where any problems are noticed, such as broken branches following high winds, the damaged part of the branch should be cut off at the appropriate time of year. This is to ensure that any decay in the branch does not spread back into the remainder of the tree. Avoid laying impervious materials near trees, especially under the canopy as this may cause damage due to a reduction in the amount of water available to the tree roots in the long term. Avoid placing timber decking around

When planting new trees ensure that they are not likely to grow too large in time for their location or that they will obscure architectural features of the house.

Trees are a valuable contribution to the urban environment and take many years to reach maturity.

trees as this prevents air from circulating and allows rot to become established that may transfer into the soil and, consequently, to the tree roots. Any disturbance of the soil underneath the canopy may affect the roots and ultimately the health of the tree. Where building works are being undertaken, trees are particularly vulnerable to damage. The area under the canopy must be fenced off, so that the soil is not compacted over the roots by vehicles, machinery or people constantly walking over them. Additional protection to tree trunks is necessary to avoid mechanical damage from vehicles or machinery since this may cause irreversible damage. Where trenches have to be dug through gardens, ensure that they are routed well away from any trees, as both the roots and trunks may be damaged in the process.

ARCHAEOLOGY

Where any disturbance of the ground is being considered, whether this is from digging trenches or in creating new garden features, a careful examination for any potential archaeology is appropriate before any works start. Even if the discoveries do not date back very far, they are a part of the history of the house and garden and may be usefully documented for the future. If anything is discovered which looks of interest, contact the local archaeological trust or the county archaeological unit. Where a house is in an area of known archaeological interest greater restrictions may apply, so speak to the planning department before carrying out any works, as permissions may be necessary before any works can begin.

This tree may have been planted at the same time that the adjoining Victorian house was built and is a part of the setting and an integral part of the history of the house.

CHAPTER 6

Expanding Living Areas

As altering or expanding living areas is becoming popular, many local authorities now have guidelines on their websites as to the scale and extent of adaptations that are in keeping with the character of particular types of older house. While a lack of space is often the main reason for considering changes, it may often be a cheaper and more environmentally friendly solution to make better use of the existing space, which would also retain more of the existing character of the house. In addition, enlarging a house is likely to lead to additional maintenance and upkeep costs in the future. There are also the environmental considerations, as new resources are consumed during any building project. New building materials consume energy in their manufacture and transportation, while existing materials have already consumed energy during their production that is known as 'embodied energy' and to discard them is wasteful in energy conservation terms. Where a house has not been altered nor extended, it will have retained more of its original features and character, beside possibly being worth more. Where there are perceived problems, there may be other easier solutions, as, for example, buying more suitable furniture (especially if it is second-hand, as new materials and energy would not need to have been used in the process). Other options might include putting items into storage, for example, to free up areas of the house.

Consider the alternative solutions seriously and with a degree of flexibility and openness of mind, before deciding whether alterations or additions are really necessary or appropriate to the future of the house. If there really are no alternative solutions, then start by assembling a budget for the works and determine what is and is not to be included within this figure. For example, are the costs of furniture and curtains included or not? Identify the best dates to have the works carried out, given that bad weather in the winter months is best avoided and necessary to avoid completely when using many traditional materials outdoors. Factor in any significant household events and avoid requiring the works to have been completed by a particular deadline as target dates for finishing the works may not be achievable if problems are discovered once the building works have started.

PROFESSIONAL HELP

Having written a brief for the works, the next stage is to appoint either an architect or a chartered building surveyor to progress the project (*see also* Chapter 2). The most important criteria is to find an architect or surveyor who fully understands older houses. This is so that they can sympathetically extend an existing house, while retaining the original fabric and its character for the future. An architect or surveyor, once appointed, would then be able to examine the problems and propose solutions. These may include alternative ideas for solving particular problems that may not necessarily involve altering or extending the existing living spaces. An architect or surveyor is able to progress the project from start to finish. Depending on the extent of the works, the input of a conservation-accredited structural engineer (see websites) may be required. Where there are complicated service requirements for the new addition a services engineer may be required. Where the value of the building project is going to be significant, then the services of a quantity surveyor may be appropriate in order to ensure that costs are properly understood and if possible kept within certain parameters. Once the design has been developed and agreed, applications for various planning and building regulations approvals may be necessary, depending on the type and scale of the proposed works and whether the house is listed or in a conservation area.

Time Scales

A building project may take at least six months for the preparation of the design drawings and their submission for a planning application. In addition, building regulations applications (called building standards in Scotland) and, where applicable, party wall awards may be required. Only once all the appropriate permissions have been granted can work start on site. The length of work on site will depend on its scope and scale. Ideally, any building works should be started in the spring during the better weather. When preparing for a building project, unforeseen situations may arise – for example, when unexpected drains or cable runs are discovered in the ground, or sudden shortages of building material occur – so be prepared for the timetable to be extended as a result.

Permissions

There are usually a number of permissions that may be necessary, depending on the nature of the works. Where a professional has been appointed they are usually able to advise on these, but the following are some of the areas that may need to be considered.

Planning Consents

Planning permission would usually be necessary, depending on the proposed works. Where a house is listed, additional consent is required for all internal and external alterations and some types of repair. Where a house is in a conservation area, depending on the types of work being proposed, they may also require conservation area consent. National Parks and Areas of Outstanding Natural Beauty (AONBs) may also have special requirements. The local authority's planning and conservation officers are a good starting point to

Expanding living spaces should be carefully considered before proceeding.

establish which consents may be necessary. Where an architect or a surveyor has been appointed, they are usually able to advise on these aspects of the project.

Covenants

Where a property has covenants placed upon it, the approval of the granting authority must be given before any building works are carried out, but the existence of any restrictive covenants should ordinarily have been identified during the legal process of buying the house.

Party Walls

Where any building works are being considered that fall within certain stated limits of adjoining buildings, then a party wall agreement has to be in place between the surveyors acting for both property owners. There is a procedure set out by government that may be as simple as an exchange of letters, or may involve two sets of surveyors. The owner who is proposing the works pays the surveyors' fees (*see* websites).

Building Regulations (England, Wales and Northern Ireland) and Building Standards (Scotland)

The building regulations/standards (*see* websites) constitute a set of technical performance requirements that cover additions or certain types of alteration to existing houses. Discuss these with your architect or surveyor or the local authority's building controls department.

Listed Buildings and VAT

Where a house is listed, if the proposed works are considered as alterations within government definitions, then VAT might be applicable at the zero rate on certain qualifying parts of them. However, the rules and requirements are complex, and where VAT amounts to a significant sum then specialist tax advice may be appropriate (*see* websites).

Building Insurance

When building works are being planned, the owner's insurance company must be notified of the dates of them, as there will be a different risk while they are in progress. Formal building contract documents usually mention insurance responsibilities and cover may need to be extended for any additional risks.

Construction (Design and Management) Regulations 2007

These are health and safety regulations (often called CDM Regs for short) designed to reduce the number of accidents involving buildings and building works. Depending on the scale of the works, the Health and Safety Executive may need to be notified (*see* websites).

Payment of Those Connected with a Building Project

Formal building contract documents as used by architects and surveyors set out clearly defined limits for the payment of contractors, usually a maximum of fourteen days. Builders usually have to purchase materials and pay staff in advance of being able to invoice the homeowner for the works. The best way for a homeowner to show his or her appreciation of the work being done is to pay invoices promptly. Where a query does arise, resolve it swiftly, otherwise this can easily detract from the future working relationship between the parties involved and the building work is likely to suffer in the process.

Protection of the House and Garden during Building Works

When a building project is being carried out, there are invariably areas not directly connected with the actual building that need to be dealt with.

An oil delivery pipe has dislodged unprotected bricks in this pier.

Connections may need to be made to existing services outside the immediate area of work, so be prepared for disruption elsewhere in the house. Gardens, trees and plants may be damaged during building works. So make sure that there is adequate protection in place, or be prepared to dig up vulnerable plants before any building works start. Gardens are likely to be compacted as people walk over them or materials stored on them. Where an architect or surveyor is overseeing the works, they should be able to specify in the contract documents areas to be protected in both the house and the garden and which areas should be identified for the storage of building materials.

Where there are trees near paths or driveways make sure that their trunks are adequately protected against damage since they may never fully recover from it. The root system of a tree under its canopy may be compacted by vehicles passing by or by pedestrians constantly walking over it, so protection here too will be necessary. Even when building works are not in progress, delivery lorries may still damage buildings, gardens or trees, so be vigilant when these situations arise.

PARTICULAR TYPES OF ALTERATION OR EXTENSION

Porches

Local authorities may have guidelines on their websites to help to inform design decisions about porches. Where a row of existing houses was originally built without them, adding one to a house would usually distort the appearance of the row. Often, a much simpler solution that is both less expensive and less disruptive is to add an internal lobby to the house. Other improvements might be to have a thermally-lined curtain, drawn over the door at night to reduce draughts. The Victorians developed clever rails that lifted a curtain when the door was opened. Additional draught-proofing may also be considered around door edges. Where the original front door is fitted within a recessed porch, adding a second, outer door breaks up the architectural rhythm of a row of houses, and adding a new canopy over a door is usually not in keeping with the surroundings, if there are similar houses within a group. When porches may be acceptable in design terms, materials that are more easily reversible may be more appropriate, such as a timber porch that would not permanently damage the wall to which it was fixed.

Where a new door has been added to the front of an open porch, it changes the emphasis of this pair of houses.

The exterior of this house appears to be very little altered and retains the original railings that were produced by the local foundry.

The addition of the porch between the two windows has changed the relationship between them.

The addition of a porch on this row of cottages changes the overall emphasis.

Kitchens

Victorian and Edwardian kitchens usually had a separate scullery, where space permitted, which contained the sink. As kitchens are usually one of the first areas to be updated when a new owner moves in, it is rare to find original kitchen fittings that have survived. However, where they do, keep them as part of the history of the house. Even kitchen fittings from a later period, regardless of how recent they are, form part of this history. While some fittings may currently be out of fashion, in ten years' time they may be the height of fashion once again. Where fittings may look dated by comparison with contemporary designs, simple alterations or enhancements may create unique results. These may range from a change of paint colour to updating work surfaces, while still retaining the original kitchen units. Older units are often more solidly constructed than those currently available.

The size of this opening indicates that the original kitchen range was located in this room and has since been replaced.

The environmental implications of replacing an existing kitchen are that the materials in it have already used up energy in their manufacture which would be wasted if these materials were thrown away. In addition, new materials would be consumed and the manufacture, energy and transportation associated with them would all contribute to further carbon emissions. If you are considering using new or natural materials such as stone or marble, consider where these materials are being transported from and how they are produced. Then consider what will happen to these materials at the end of their life, when they wear out or go out of fashion and how they would be recycled. Before embarking on a scheme to enlarge or alter a kitchen, consider what are the benefits of the current layout; often it is less stressful and cheaper to alter present lifestyles to suit the existing kitchen, rather than physically altering the kitchen.

Larger kitchens are more costly to heat, so consider what might happen in the future. For example, if the size of a household is smaller in the future, large rooms may not be so appropriate. In addition, keeping the existing room layouts ensures that the integrity of the original house plan is maintained. There are many benefits in retaining separate areas, rather than incorporating them into larger ones. Retaining an existing pantry may reduce the need to refrigerate or store food in the kitchen, while using an original scullery for washing may reduce noise levels and improve hygiene within the kitchen. Where a house is listed, alterations are likely to require listed building consent and building regulation approval may also be necessary, depending on the proposed works (*see* websites).

Bathrooms

While many earlier houses during this period were built without bathrooms in styles familiar to us today, there may still be some original or early fittings that still exist. High-level toilet or WC cisterns were popular before the arrival of more recent, low-level cisterns in the mid-twentieth century. Consider keeping the existing fittings, even if they are modern and currently out of fashion, as they may soon be back in fashion. The reason for this is that gravity gives a low-volume flush a good boost and can save water. Furthermore, any fittings that are now removed would have to be responsibly recycled if they are removed from the house. Often the addition of accessories or the changing of the colour of the walls has a far more dramatic effect on a room than changing the fittings. Where a separate room for the WC still exists, consider retaining this arrangement as current trends are moving away from including WCs in bathrooms.

While there is considerable attention being placed on increasing the number of bathrooms in houses, unless extensions are also being considered, they reduce the amount of available living accommodation. Bathrooms require a high level of servicing such as soil pipes and hot and cold water pipes. This means that to introduce new bathrooms inevitably creates disruption to other parts of the house, as connections are necessary into the existing services. In addition, new drainage trenches may need to be

This is a cast-iron, high-level toilet or WC cistern. Note also the traditional lampshade which has been easily converted to an energy-saving lamp.

This was a popular design for brackets that originally supported a high-level WC cistern.

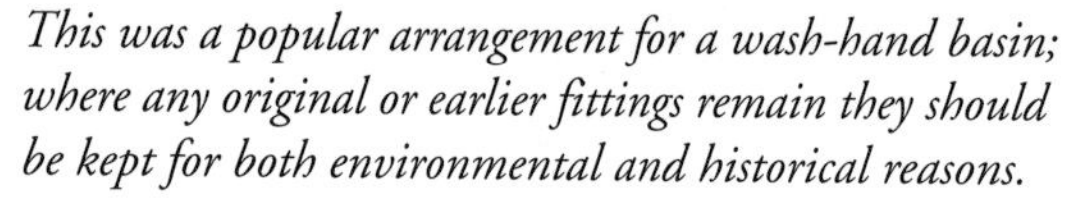

This was a popular arrangement for a wash-hand basin; where any original or earlier fittings remain they should be kept for both environmental and historical reasons.

Consider where pipes may run on the exterior of a house for new plumbing since they are likely to be less visible on the rear elevation.

dug to connect to the existing sewers. Victorian and Edwardian houses were designed so that service pipes were positioned on rear elevations, so avoid introducing external pipes on to the front or prominent elevations of a house as they may detract from the overall appearance of the house. Another consideration in connection with current trends in water and energy conservation is that in the future a house with several bathrooms may be perceived as a liability rather than the asset that they were intended to be.

Attics

Where these are accessible, they are often used for storage, but bulky items may impede the flow of air across the roof space, so be careful where such items are placed in an attic. If you are considering boarding over the attic floor, ensure that the existing ceiling joists can accommodate the additional weight of the boarding and any extra loading that may be placed on it, as building regulations/standards approval may be required (*see* websites). Where there is any existing insulation, it is important to keep an air gap at the eaves, to allow air to circulate, so that any dampness in the roof timbers is able to dry out naturally. Where extra living accommodation is required within a house, the attic is usually the first area to be identified for conversion. Specialist companies often carry out this type of work. Employing an architect to design a bespoke solution may seem more costly but it should ensure that a tailor-made and more imaginatively designed space is created. Planning and listed building consent, where a house is listed, together with conservation area consent in conservation areas, party wall awards and buildings regulations approval give an idea of the consents that may be required, depending on the proposed scale of the works. Where an additional storey is being added to a house for living accommodation, there may be fire prevention implications for the rest of the house. This may mean that fire-resisting doors and high-level escape windows are required under the building regulations/standards.

A group of houses with roof extensions.

Alterations should respect the original and add to rather than detract from its appeal.

Temporary roofs may be necessary when attics are being converted.

A cellar conversion in progress.

Basement excavations usually require a considerable amount of soil to be removed from the house.

Cellars

Many houses may have a cellar, as this was where coal was stored for use in the kitchen range and on open fires. But creating living accommodation out of a cellar is now becoming a popular way of increasing the size of the house. These types of conversion are usually carried out by specialist contractors because there may be significant engineering requirements in terms of underpinning party walls. Where existing cellars are being enlarged or new basement rooms created, this may involve the removal of large quantities of soil. Planning permission may be necessary, as

This cellar conversion has a small window installed rather than the front garden having been excavated to create a larger window.

Where a light well is created in the front garden, protection must be provided against falls.

Basement conversions may be overlooked from the street, so screening with plants may be appropriate, but this may also reduce the amount of light entering these rooms.

well as party wall awards and other consents depending on whether the house is listed or in a conservation area and on the scale and design of the proposed conversion. Commissioning an architect to create a living area in the basement may ensure a unique solution to the problem, rather that a standardized one from a company that specializes in this type of conversion.

Conservatories and Garden Rooms

Where early or original conservatories still exist they are usually made of timber and may retain original glass in the windows as well as original floor tiles. If these elements survive they should be carefully repaired and maintained for the future benefit of the house.

Old photographs or maps may identify where conservatories that were attached to the house or within the garden may have been demolished. Traditionally, conservatories were made of painted timber or perhaps cast-iron sections. Stained or decorative glass may have been used in some or all of the windows, while plain glass was more likely to have been used where the conservatory was a more functional area for growing plants. The floors may have been tiled and remains of them may be found, even if the conservatory itself has long since been demolished. Random marks or the remains of limewash on an existing wall may indicate where the junctions might have been between former glasshouses and walls.

North-facing conservatories were often used as ferneries. Adding conservatories to existing houses as

Existing conservatories are a part of the history of the house, regardless of their age.

These houses have had a similar type of extension installed adjoining their boundary walls.

living rooms rather than for growing exotic plants has been popular for the last few decades. However, with the increasing standards of energy conservation that are now necessary, 'garden rooms' are now becoming more popular, as they have more areas of solid walls and less glazing. In addition, garden rooms, having solid roofs, may reduce problems that could arise from being overlooked by neighbours, and also reduce light pollution towards neighbouring properties. Where space allows, the location of any new conservatory or garden room should enhance the setting of the house rather than detract from the original design. New additions should generally be a subservient feature of the existing house, rather that being too dominant. Planning permission and building regulations approvals are usually required for such additions, and where a house is listed or in a conservation area, additional permissions would be necessary.

CHAPTER 7

Energy Conservation

The conserving of energy and looking after old houses in a considerate way are often achievable together. They are both about avoiding the waste of existing resources and building materials, which is more sustainable behaviour than replacing parts of the existing house with new materials. To introduce new materials into an existing house uses up additional energy during both their manufacture and transportation. In addition, any existing materials that are thrown away during building work mean that the energy consumed during their production is wasted. Before a house is put up for sale a Home Information Pack (HIP), known as a Purchaser's Information Pack (PIP) in Scotland, has to be prepared (*see* websites). Also as part of this documentation an Energy Performance Certificate has to be completed, which gives an indication of the potential energy consumption of the house. The rating system used for assessing the energy use is similar to that already in use for domestic appliances such as refrigerators and freezers. It is based on the potential use of energy in assumed conditions, and so would not account for frugality on one hand or excess on the other.

Many energy conservation measures can be introduced into older houses without the appearance of the house being altered.

Saving Money and Energy

There are many, often simple measures, that can be adopted when living in a Victorian or Edwardian house to save energy and money. The following sections give examples that range in cost and complexity. But, as a starting point, before spending any money on improving the energy efficiency of the house, ensure that the house is used as efficiently as possible as it is. This means making sure that the consumption of existing resources is reduced to a minimum by examining the ways in which the house is currently used to see where improvements might be made. It is often small adjustments to a lifestyle that can make quite a considerable difference. For example, make sure that curtains or shutters (where they exist) are always closed at dusk, especially in heated rooms, and are opened only during the day. Where a room is on a north-facing wall, try to keep the curtains or shutters closed when the room is not in use, as they act as a secondary layer of insulation and retain more heat within the house.

Vertical sliding shutters may retain more heat than curtains, especially when there is a radiator in front of the window.

Try to only heat rooms that are actually going to be used, so decide which rooms these are and when. Make sure that doors to rooms are kept shut, as this is likely to make a considerable difference to the amount of heat that is retained within a particular room. Turning down both the temperature of the boiler and any room thermostats by a number of degrees is likely to make a big difference to energy consumption and reduce fuel bills. Then consider what additional heat generating sources are located within each room, such as boilers, dishwashers, heating or hot water pipes, as these generate background heat that may be conserved by keeping the doors to these rooms closed. Where an open fire is not being used, make sure that the flue opening is covered to reduce the amount of heat that escapes up the flue. In addition to looking at the house, think about wearing warmer clothing or more layers to keep warmer.

Small-cost DIY Works

Make sure that any large gaps between doors or windows and their frames are draught-proofed. Applying draught strip around the edges of doors or windows is an efficient way of reducing draughts. A more temporary measure may be to make up fabric rolls that can be laid over the meeting rail between sash windows or laid at the bottom of doors to stop draughts. These can then be removed during the summer months to allow for greater ventilation.

During the winter months ensure that any fireplaces that are not going to be used have their flues covered. Any flue stoppers should be carefully taken out during the summer months to allow air to circulate within the flue to allow any dampness to dry out.

Where a house has existing shutters that have been boarded up or are not in use (often due to layers of paint having clogged them up), it is usually fairly easy to remove any boards or paint that are stopping them from working. Shutters can reduce the amount of heat loss from a room, so where possible try to bring them back into use and close them at dusk.

Where windows do not have shutters, make sure that they have fabric blinds or, at the very least, thin, voile-type curtains that can be drawn during cold days to reduce heat loss through single glazing. At dusk, more layers of curtaining can be drawn over the windows to retain heat. Ideally, curtains should be lined with as many layers of interlining as possible that include thermal linings. There are now available perforated, foil-based fabric thermal linings to increase heat reflection.

Try to ensure that all external doors have door curtains to reduce draughts and consequently heat loss, and make sure that these curtains are well insulated with plenty of layers of interlining. Door curtains can also be used over internal doors to reduce the heat loss between adjoining rooms and be removable during the summer months, as appropriate.

Temporary secondary glazing for the winter months can be put over roof lights or windows. This can be carried out by using DIY kits that include thin, flexible, clear plastic sheets that can be stretched over the inside of the window. Alternatively, a lightweight timber framework may be used to fit the opening, to which plastic bubble wrap can be attached, preferably in at least two layers. While neither option is particularly elegant, they are reversible as well as being a cheap and easy means of conserving heat. Heat loss is far greater through roof lights than from any other type of window, so make sure that they are the first windows to be fitted with secondary glazing.

Fitting surface-mounted door closers to internal and external doors is likely to reduce heat loss further, but choose the device carefully to try to ensure that parts of the door or frame are not cut out to accommodate the closer. Such devices may also be removed during the summer months if desired.

Existing hot water cylinders should have insulation jackets around them and, if space permits, consider fitting another jacket for additional insulation. Cold-water storage tanks in roof spaces should be insulated to ensure that they do not freeze in winter, since this could lead to burst pipes when they start to thaw out. Hot and cold water pipes should be lagged to avoid heat loss or burst pipes. If there are high-level toilet cisterns on external walls these may be prone to freezing in very cold weather. One option may be to incorporate insulation on to the surface of the wall

This door curtain has been made from an old bedspread interlined with a blanket to provide good insulation over a north-facing door.

Applying secondary glazing to roof lights, even if they are later replacements, as in this example or already double-glazed, will reduce the amount of heat loss.

Where the metal escutcheon plate, a cover which swings over a keyhole, is missing it is sensible to reinstate it to reduce draughts.

This is a modern mortise lock set within the thickness of the door, with an escutcheon plate cover in position.

behind the cistern to help in maintaining a higher local temperature.

When existing light bulbs come to the end of their life this is the point at which to replace them with energy-efficient lamps. Due to their size, not all existing light fittings may be able to accommodate them. And also check that where dimmer switches, movement detectors or light sensors switch on the lights, they are compatible with these types of lamp.

Roof spaces above bedroom ceilings should be insulated where possible to at least the thickness as currently specified in the building regulations/standards (*see* websites). When introducing insulation or additional layers of insulation, care must be taken not to seal up ventilation paths across roof spaces as these allow air to circulate around the roof timbers and keep them from decaying. Ventilation takes moist air away, which reduces the risk of damage from beetles or rot from becoming established in the timbers. Where there is a cold water storage tank in a roof space this should also be insulated; but it is sensible not to put insulation under the tank, so that a small amount of heat is allowed to rise up from the room below to keep the tank from freezing. Other smaller areas to insulate are the roof side of access hatches and elsewhere in the house, the inner face of letterboxes, where a metal or fabric inner flap can be fixed over them.

Keyholes and cat flaps are further examples of where heat may also be lost. In addition, consider such items as overflow pipes from toilet cisterns that allow warmed air to escape from the house. Cistern lids should be tightly fitting to reduce the draught, but do not block the overflow pipe itself as this may cause problems if the ball valve in the toilet cistern ever becomes defective.

Ensure that loft or access hatches are insulated on the upper surface and that draught seals are added around their edges to reduce heat loss from heated areas. Some of these hatches may also need to be fire-protected as well.

Medium-expense Items

Where a house has missing shutters, to have new ones made to fit the openings is sensible. The heat loss within the room will be reduced if they are closed at dusk, so that more heat is retained within the room. Sometimes shutters were stored in the house after they had been taken down, so look in out-of-the-way storage areas, just in case the original shutters are still around. If replacement shutters are the only option, try to see what designs were used in any similar, neighbouring houses. A local joiner should then be able to make new shutters of a similar design. Ensure that when new shutters are being fitted that none of the original fabric of the house has to be cut away or removed to accommodate them.

Where the existing radiator system does not have thermostatic radiator valves already fitted to each radiator, it may be possible to have these installed. However, with some old systems the existing radiators may never become sufficiently hot to justify the installation of such valves. Where any alterations are being proposed this may mean that the whole of the radiator system has to be drained down, so a certain amount of upheaval may be involved. In addition, there are no guarantees that thermostatic radiator valves can be fitted to every radiator, and this may not be easy where older iron pipes are involved. Finding a plumber who has had experience of successfully installing these valves on an existing and often elderly heating system is the most important consideration. In addition, ensure that the design and location of new valves has been agreed beforehand since some are bulky and less attractive than others.

Laying carpets and underlays that have a breathable backing should insulate the floors against draughts and, as they are breathable, this allows some air to circulate to the underlying floorboards. Try to avoid laying foam-backed carpets or foam underlays as these do not allow the underlying timber floor structure to breathe. Leaving gaps between and around floorboards exposed is likely to increase the amount of heat loss through ground floors.

Consider the location of the house in relation to the prevailing wind as it may be sensible to think about growing some trees or shrubs (but not too close to the house) that might act as a wind break to reduce the draughts entering the house in the first place.

Fan pressurization tests are used on new buildings to establish if and where there are any air leaks so that these can be reduced to comply with current building regulations/standards (see websites). These tests can also be used on older houses, but be aware that a certain amount of ventilation is necessary in older houses to allow any dampness to dry out, since sealing up older houses is not a good idea as it can lead to dampness, with the consequence that rot and decay may become established (*see* Chapter 2).

More Expensive Items

When a boiler gets to the stage that it is uneconomic to repair it is the time to consider replacing it. If the boiler is to be replaced by an oil or gas boiler it is now mandatory for the replacement to be a condensing boiler. These are designed to be as efficient as possible by extracting heat from the exhaust gases. In addition, boilers can also be 'combination' boilers, where domestic hot water is generated within the boiler at the moment it is required, rather than being stored in a hot water cylinder for later use. The installation of a combination boiler is likely to require that the existing pipework in the house is altered or adapted, which may involve some upheaval. The installation of a combination boiler may mean that both the hot water storage cylinder and possibly an attic cold

Modern boiler flues can produce quite noticeable plumes.

water tank may no longer be required. Existing storage tanks might possibly be suitable for reuse for grey-water recycling or rain-water harvesting (see below). Unless an existing boiler has come to the end of its usable life, replacing it earlier is going to use up more resources in the manufacture and installation of a new one, which being more complex might have a shorter service life. Where new condensing boilers are used they create a white vapour plume. There are requirements about where flues may be sited under the current building regulations/standards (*see* websites), but be aware that the steam that these boilers produce may have an adverse affect on surrounding building materials such as thatch, as lichens may be attracted to the area above the flue, for example.

Secondary glazing for existing windows is another element to consider. Rather than buying standard, off-the-peg frames, try to find a local joiner able to make up timber secondary window frames that can be fitted during the winter months and removed during the summer, if required. Fitting secondary glazing to roof lights and north-facing windows should take priority, as this is where the greatest amount of heat loss is likely to occur. It may be far more preferable to fit secondary glazing to windows rather than replace the windows with double glazing. Replacing windows can be detrimental to the external appearance of an old house, and, where one is listed or in a conservation area, permission is unlikely to be granted for such an alteration. The original timber windows and glass would be lost, more natural resources would be consumed and other resources wasted. In addition, secondary glazing has the potential to reduce sound transmission more than some double glazing. But fitting secondary glazing to existing windows might perhaps be more difficult where the windows have shutters. When any additional elements are being fitted to a window, make sure that none of the existing timberwork has to be removed to accommodate them, also make sure that, where intermediate glazing bars are necessary on secondary glazing, that they line through with those on the existing windows, otherwise they will look out of place on the exterior. Where a house is listed, consents may be required, so speak to the local conservation officer.

New Technologies

There are an increasing number of new technologies that are becoming available to homeowners that harness the sun, wind or heat from the earth. Most of these require considerable capital outlay, which may take many years to repay when balanced against reduced fuel bills. There may be grants available to help to offset the initial costs (*see* websites). Depending on the type of new technology being considered, planning approvals and other consents may be required, so again speak to the local authority.

Solar Panels

Solar panels are primarily used for heating water in a hot water cylinder. The solar-heated water is passed through the hot water cylinder in a pipe coil to transfer heat to the water in the cylinder. This is known as an indirect system as the heat rather than the water from the panels is transferred into the hot water cylinder. When considering fitting solar panels to a house, the most important visual consideration is to try to ensure that they do not detract from its appearance. Solar collectors to produce hot water may be made from either flat glass-fronted panels or from rows of glass tubes containing pipes. The latter

Positioning solar panels on the rear elevation is usually less visually obtrusive.

The positioning of these solar panels on the front of this house draws attention away from the surrounding architectural features. Listed houses and those in conservation areas usually require permission for such installations, so speak to the conservation office in the local authority.

are likely to be the more efficient but more expensive to buy. The panels are ideally placed so that they face direct into the sun, but the main front roof may often be too obtrusive visually. A south-facing roof is often at a good angle to catch the sun and has an unobstructed view, but roofs are not the only locations that are suitable and other locations may give the potential to alter the angle to suit the sun at different times of year. These systems usually require additions to an existing hot water cylinder or to a replacement cylinder to incorporate the extra pipework from the solar panel, in addition to the conventional heating coil. Because this type of system uses a hot water cylinder to store heated water, this means that these types of system are not appropriate where a combination boiler is to be used. This is because these boilers heat water direct from the cold water main for immediate use, rather than heating water that is then stored for later use. Routes for the new pipes should be planned in advance, so that they are located as discreetly as possible within the existing house. Depending on the type of installation proposed in a house, permissions may be required, especially where a house is listed or in conservation area, so speak to the conservation office at the local authority.

Photovoltaic Panels (PVs)

These are a particular type of solar collector used where electricity is to be generated rather than hot water. These systems are usually more expensive than solar water heating panels due to the technology involved. They are usually placed on roofs or used as vertical panels facing the sun. Further developments are likely to make them more efficient and easier to disguise in the future. Solar-powered garden lights are a familiar form of photovoltaic panels. There are usually considerable capital costs involved in manufacturing the panels, so it is best to place them where they are unlikely to be damaged. Where a house is listed or in conservation area consents are usually required.

Wind Turbines

These have become fashionable since DIY stores began selling them, but the energy consumed in their manufacture, transportation and installation means that the payback period may be significant for the amount of electricity generated. Furthermore, the visual impact of a turbine has to be carefully considered in relation to the house and its surroundings. They have to be sited away from trees or obstructions that might reduce the potential wind speed. In urban areas there may be insufficient wind or too many gusts for them to operate efficiently. Where a turbine has to be located away from a house the cables that run between it and the house have to be buried and there may be a drop in power as a result. Noise levels and structural vibration may also be issues. Locating a wind turbine on one house in a row may affect the appearance of them all. Depending on the size and position of the turbines and whether the house is listed or in a conservation area consents will usually be required, so speak to the conservation office at the local authority.

Biomass-fuelled Boilers

There is currently an increasing range of boiler fuels, beyond the traditional supplies of solid fuel, oil and gas. One such is biomass fuel, which is based on plant or animal material. The materials range from tree cuttings to farm waste (such as chicken manure), but for domestic use the most readily available fuel sources are likely to be wood chips, wood pellets or logs. Where these types of fuel are being considered, there are usually additional factors to be borne in mind, such as transportation distances and storage arrangements. These criteria have to be balanced against the fact that the amount of carbon dioxide released when the fuel is burnt is believed to be similar to that absorbed when the trees were growing. Depending on the type of fuel being considered (and the visual impact of a flue), there may be local restrictions in place. Burning wood in urban areas needs to be efficiently controlled to avoid the contravention of smoke-control legislation since the straightforward burning of timber can create too much smoke (*see* websites).

Boilers like these are specially designed to take logs.

Combined Heat and Power (CHP) Units

Combined heat and power units are now growing in popularity, although they have been available for a while. They work by making use of surplus heat from a central heating boiler to drive a simple generator to produce electricity. While these are relatively new to this country, the idea is likely to gain ground as units become available in a greater range of capacities. An advantage of generating electricity directly in the home is that transmission losses are eliminated. The offsetting provided by the electricity generation may be a practical way to accommodate the extra heating needed by older buildings that simply cannot be insulated to a high standard.

Ground-source Heat Pumps

These have become popular for heating in recent years and are well established in other parts of Europe. They work by drawing low levels of heat either from below ground level, from the air or from a stream. This heat is in effect concentrated by the action of the heat pump, using electricity, so that low-grade heat carried into the heat pump by means of piped liquid, can be converted into higher-grade heat and transferred to the water that circulates to heat the house via radiators. This system works on a similar principle to a refrigerator that takes heat from food and transfers it outside. The pipes that are used to collect low level heat from the ground may require an extensive area of them to be laid out below the ground. Where there is insufficient space to lay these pipes horizontally, vertical pipes may be used instead that have to be sunk much deeper into the ground in boreholes. Care is needed in case the excavations disturb any hidden archaeological materials, so speak to the local conservation officer.

To convert the energy into usable heat requires a unit about the size of a large domestic refrigerator to which pipes bringing low-grade heat from the garden (or the air or a stream) are attached, and from the unit pipes flow out taking the 'concentrated' heat to underfloor heating or radiators. There is a capital cost involved in fitting these installations. They require a well-insulated house and are said to work best with underfloor heating because these use low levels of heating. But the installation of underfloor heating can be problematic in an older house (*see* Chapter 4), though the system may be able to work with big, old-fashioned Victorian radiators that were designed to use water of a relatively low temperature. A well-balanced system may get about two units of 'free' heat for every unit of electricity consumed, but the systems need to be carefully balanced and the house to be capable of a high level of insulation for the full benefits to be gained. This heat is not entirely free, as a significant proportion of it is paid for in electricity.

A water butt is rainwater harvesting at it simplest. Choose one that fits the setting and ensure that it has an overflow pipe to prevent it from getting too full and soaking nearby walls.

Rainwater Harvesting

The simplest and most long-standing form of this is a water butt filled from a rainwater pipe. However, underground or perhaps attic tanks can be installed to store rainwater for later use within in the house where it is not suitable for uses such as drinking but can be used for flushing WCs and for some washing machines; however, it would require filtering and a basic level of treatment to avoid the minute plant and animal life that exists in water butts. Where the water has to be pumped to locations around the house or garden this may defeat the object of reducing the total energy and resources consumption.

Grey-water Recycling

This is the term used for reusing water from basins, dishwashers, washing machines and baths (water that has been used in sinks and WCs is known as black water). To store grey water in an existing house requires a storage tank, additional pipes and an electric pump to pump the water upwards to appliances below the level of the storage tank. Where storage tanks are to be located outside the house and above ground, they have to be carefully sited so that they do not detract from the setting of the house. It might be possible to reuse redundant cold water storage tanks where an existing boiler has been replaced with a combination boiler (*see* earlier in this chapter). Once the water has been filtered, treated to some extent to control bacteria and stored, it can be used for flushing WCs or some gardening uses. However, the amount of new equipment and electricity that may be necessary to take advantage of grey water may mean that it may be more sustainable simply to try to reduce the amount of water used in the first place.

APPENDIX I

House Maintenance Checklist

Planning maintenance activities in advance ensures that there are no unexpected surprises. The best times to look over the house are in the spring, after the worst of the winter weather is over, and again in the autumn, when leaves might have blocked gutters and drains. The following are some key aspects to look at around the house.

Ensure that creepers are cut back regularly, and especially in the autumn, so that they do not block gutters.

Rainwater disposal system

- Check that all gutters and downpipes are running freely.
- Check that all gullies at ground level are clear and free-flowing.

Chimneys and roof

- Check the condition of chimneys and roof coverings by looking at them through binoculars.
- Where possible, check the condition of the roof from the attic.

Walls

- Check for signs of any defects, such as cracks in masonry or blistering paintwork.
- Check over all paintwork and repaint as necessary, or at least keep cracks in window putty and on cills filled and painted until the next decoration.

Services

- Check all pipes, both those fitted on the outside of the house as well as all internal ones, for signs of leaks.

Ventilation

- Check that air bricks to underfloor spaces have not become blocked.
- Check that ventilation paths within roofs have not become blocked.

Ensure that air vents are kept clear of obstructions so that air is able to circulate freely under floorboards and around cellars.

Water taps and pipes

- Turn off outside taps at the internal isolating valve during winter.
- Insulate any exposed pipes outside and in unheated areas to prevent damage from freezing.

Around the house

- Check the junction between the base of the house wall and the surrounding surfaces for any signs of defects, such as dampness or damaged areas of wall surfaces.

Around the garden

- Check trees, fences and walls for signs of weakness or damage, especially after high winds or torrential downpours.

A planned list of maintenance actions can help to keep a house healthy.

APPENDIX II

Mistakes to Avoid with a Victorian or an Edwardian House

EXTERIOR

- Applying paint or render over original brick or stone walls.
- Replacing rather than repairing original doors or windows.
- Changing from the original material used for roof covering.
- Replacing cast-iron guttering with plastic.
- Cleaning the brick or stonework on just one house within a group.
- Applying non-breathable paints or finishes to the exterior of the house.
- Insensitive alterations or extensions.
- Removing original paths, walls, railings or hedges from around the house.
- Replacing original glass.
- Inappropriate location of television aerials, satellite dishes or soil stacks.

INTERIOR

- Removing any original features, fittings or surfaces.
- Sanding or stripping wooden flooring.
- Sanding or stripping paint from doors, windows and other timber features.
- Removing internal partitions or walls to create an open-plan house.
- Damaging lath and plaster with modern wall fixings or downlighters.
- Insensitive installations of pipework and cables.
- Sealing up of breathable surfaces with modern impervious finishes.

Websites

For updates see: www.oldhouse.info

AMENITY SOCIETIES

The Victorian Society
www.victorian-society.org.uk

ARCHAEOLOGY

The Council for British Archaeology
www.britarch.ac.uk

The Council for Scottish Archaeology
www.scottisharchaeology.org.uk

The Institute of Field Archaeologists
www.archaeologists.net

BATS

Bat Conservation Trust
www.bats.org.uk

Cyngor Cefn Gwlad Cymru (The Countryside Council for Wales)
www.ccw.gov.uk

Northern Ireland Environment Agency
www.ni-environment.gov.uk

Natural England
www.naturalengland.org.uk

Scottish Natural Heritage
www.snh.org.uk

BIRDS

The Royal Society for the Protection of Birds
www.rspb.org.uk

BUILDING CONTRACTS

RIBA Bookshop
www.architecture.com

CONSUMER SAFETY ORGANIZATIONS

Gas
www.trustcorgi.com

Electricity
www.niceic.org.uk

Water
www.water.org.uk

ENERGY PERFORMANCE CERTIFICATES

Home information packs
www.homeinformationpacks.gov.uk

Northern Ireland
www.dfpni.gov.uk

GARDENS

The Garden History Society
www.gardenhistorysociety.org

GOVERNMENT AGENCIES

Local authority websites

Cadw (Wales)
www.cadw.wales.gov.uk

English Heritage
www.english-heritage.org.uk

Northern Ireland Environment Agency
www.ni-environment.gov.uk

Historic Scotland
www.historic-scotland.gov.uk

National Parks
www.nationalparks.gov.uk

HEALTH AND SAFETY

Construction Design and Management Regulations 2007 (CDM)
www.hse.gov.uk

Health and Safety Executive
www.hse.gov.uk

Asbestos
www.hse.gov.uk

Ladders
www.hse.gov.uk

Lead paint
www.defra.gov.uk

Lead water pipes
www.dwi.gov.uk

Lime
www.hse.gov.uk

HOME INFORMATION PACKS (HIPS)

England and Wales
www.homeinformationpacks.gov.uk

Purchaser's Information Packs (PIPS) in Scotland
www.scotland.gov.uk

NEW TECHNOLOGIES GRANTS

www.lowcarbonbuildings.org.uk

PARTY WALL ACT

www.communities.gov.uk

PLANNING, TREES AND BUILDING CONTROL

Local authorities websites

England and Wales
www.planningportal.gov.uk

Northern Ireland Environment Agency
www.ni-environment.gov.uk

Scottish building standards
www.sbsa.gov.uk

Listed Buildings: Planning Policy Guidance 15: Planning and the historic environment
www.communities.gov.uk

Satellite dishes
www.communities.gov.uk

PROFESSIONAL BODIES

Architects Accredited in Building Conservation (AABC)
www.aabc-register.co.uk

Architects Registration Board (ARB)
www.arb.org.uk

Royal Institute of British Architects (RIBA)
www.architecture.com

Royal Incorporation of Architects in Scotland (RIAS) www.rias.org.uk

Royal Society of Architects in Wales (RSAW)
www.architecture.com

Royal Society of Ulster Architects (RSUA)
www.rsua.org.uk

Royal Institution of Chartered Surveyors (RICS)
www.rics.org.uk

Conservation Accreditation Register for Engineers (CARE)
www.ice.org.uk

Institution of Civil Engineers (ICE)
www.ice.org.uk

Institution of Structural Engineers (IStructE)
www.istructe.org.uk

TAXATION

HM Revenue & Customs and VAT
www.hmrc.gov.uk

Index